...typical seer, Vyas... ...added to the *Mahabharata* or expanded out of it in approximately the third century BCE. It deals with questions of social and religious duty, the nature of action, freedom of choice, routes to spiritual liberation, and the relationship of human beings to God in a period of uncertainty and transition. From early in its history the *Bhagavad Gita* was an important focus for commentators, and later it became a source text for devotional movements. It continues to inspire a wide variety of interpretations, both within India and beyond, and it has become the most widely read Hindu religious text in the Western world.

W. J. Johnson was educated at the University of Sussex and Wolfson College, Oxford, where he was Michael Coulson Research Fellow in Indology from 1991 to 1992. He is now Lecturer in Religious Studies at the University of Wales, College of Cardiff. His major research interests are in the field of Jaina doctrine and practice.

THE WORLD'S CLASSICS

THE BHAGAVAD GITA

The *Bhagavad Gita* is a self-contained episode in the great Indian Sanskrit epic, the *Mahabharata*. The nature of its authorship and the means by which it acquired its present form are uncertain, although from internal evidence it is attributed, like the rest of the epic, to the prototypical seer, Vyasa. It may have been added to the *Mahabharata* or expanded out of it in approximately the third century B.C. It deals with questions of social and religious duty, the nature of action, freedom of choice, routes to spiritual liberation, and the relationship of human beings to God in a period of uncertainty and transition. From early in its history the *Bhagavad Gita* was an important focus for commentators, and later it became a source text for devotional movements. It continues to inspire a wide variety of interpretations, both within India and beyond, and it has become the most widely read Hindu religious text in the Western world.

W. J. Johnson was educated at the University of Sussex and Wolfson College, Oxford, where he was Michael Coulson Research Fellow in Indology from 1991 to 1992. He is now Lecturer in Religious Studies at the University of Wales College of Cardiff. His major research interests are in the field of Jaina doctrine and practice.

THE WORLD'S CLASSICS

The Bhagavad Gita

Translated with an Introduction and Notes by

W. J. JOHNSON

Oxford New York

OXFORD UNIVERSITY PRESS

Oxford University Press, Walton Street, Oxford OX2 6DP

Oxford New York
Athens Auckland Bangkok Bombay
Calcutta Cape Town Dar es Salaam Delhi
Florence Hong Kong Istanbul Karachi
Kuala Lumpur Madras Madrid Melbourne
Mexico City Nairobi Paris Singapore
Taipei Tokyo Toronto

and associated companies in
Berlin Ibadan

Oxford is a trade mark of Oxford University Press

First published as a World's Classics paperback 1994

British Library Cataloguing in Publication Data
Data available

Library of Congress Cataloging in Publication Data
Bhagavadgītā. English
Bhagavad Gita / translated with an introduction and notes by W. J. Johnson.
p. cm.
Includes bibliographical references.
I. Johnson, W. J.
BL1138.62.E5 1994 294.5'924—dc20 93-40558
ISBN 0-19-282952-1

3 5 7 9 10 8 6 4

Printed in Great Britain by
BPC Paperbacks Ltd
Aylesbury, Bucks

CONTENTS

Introduction vii

Note on the Text and Translation xx

Select Bibliography xxii

Note on Metre xxiv

Note on Typography in Chapter 1 xxv

BHAGAVAD GITA 1

Explanatory Notes 83

Note on the Pronunciation of Sanskrit Names 89

List of Sanskrit Names and Terms 91

INTRODUCTION

The *Bhagavad Gita* ('Song of the Lord') is a self-contained episode of seven hundred verses embedded in one book of the great Sanskrit epic, the *Mahabharata*. Although the *Gita* is probably over two thousand years old, Charles Wilkins's English version of 1785 was the first full translation into a modern European language. Since then, in a wide variety of translations and interpretations, it has come to represent Hinduism, and even Indian spirituality in general, to the non-specialist Western reader. It is also the archetype of that necessarily modern phenomenon, the classic of world spirituality. Over the same period the *Gita* has assumed for many Hindus a universal status, so that it is regarded not only as *the* quintessential Hindu religious text, but also as a charter for all kinds of frequently conflicting social and political action.

One reason for the *Gita*'s universality is its capacity to bear almost any shade of interpretation, because of the variegated nature of its contents. It is as though the famous epigram directed by the *Mahabharata* at itself—'What is here may be found elsewhere, what is not here is nowhere at all'—has come to be applied as a hermeneutical principle to its offspring. While this demonstrates the fact that the *Gita* is and always has been a live religious text, with an apparently limitless capacity to inspire new and necessarily valid meanings, from the perspective of the tradition in which they are coined, it does not imply that all interpretations are equally convincing from the historical and philological perspectives; far from it. Nevertheless, it is often easier for scholarly exegetes and historians (themselves not always immune to bias) to reject other interpretations than to provide totally convincing replacements.

A reason for this has already been hinted at: the *Gita* is a religious text, not a philosophical tract. Its purpose is to engender and consolidate certain attitudes in its audience, in much the same way as the 'Lord' of the title, Krishna, attempts in a variety of ways to lead his interlocutor, Arjuna, from perplexity to understanding and correct action. Although, in the context of the *Mahabharata* the problem is faced by one of the protagonists, Arjuna, and its resolution allows the action to proceed, for most Hindus the *Gita* is not simply part of the epic story but a religious teaching, transmitted to them personally by the guru-God Krishna. The problem therefore is not remote or fictional but imminent, and the solution, through the grace of God, is equally accessible.

That it is thought to be the word of God and also part of a narrative encompassing, in the words of a Western theatrical adaptation of the *Mahabharata*, 'the poetical history of mankind',[1] helps us to understand what seems to be a paradoxical fact about the *Gita*, in the light of its recent history. Although it has been revered and the object of much exegesis from early in its existence, detailed knowledge of its contents seems not to have penetrated beyond scholarly circles in India until the last hundred years. One reason for this is that the original language of the *Gita*, Sanskrit, was known only to a relatively small number of *pandits*; moreover, translations into modern Indian languages, even if considered desirable, would have required a readership, which in turn required education. Literacy of that kind began to appear in India on a significant scale only in the nineteenth century, initially through the medium of English. Furthermore, it was not until this period that printing presses were introduced, creating the possibility of the widespread distribution of written material.

Before this change, it seems likely that most Indians, if they knew the *Gita* at all, knew it as part of an orally transmitted and flexible narrative tradition, as an adjunct to various rituals, and as material for recitation in a devotional context. In other words, they might have known and been able to recite certain verses, but they would have had no theological overview of the text. Indeed, for many Hindus the situation may not be so very different today: what the *Gita* is (the word of God) or what it is perceived to represent (the values inherent in Hindu culture) may be more important than its literal, verse by verse meaning. Moreover, its primary meaning may not be in its metaphysical

[1] Jean-Claude Carrière (translated Peter Brook), *The Mahabharata: A Play Based upon the Indian Classical Epic* (London: Methuen, 1987), p.3.

or philosophical content at all, but in the story it tells, and in the relationship it dramatizes between God and human beings.

This is not intended as a denial of the evident fact that some of the *Gita*'s teachings have, in a generalized form, become cornerstones of belief for many, if not most Hindus. But it may serve as a warning to the modern Westerner, picking up a book called *The Bhagavad Gita* and reading it from cover to cover, not to assume that she or he is using, understanding, or valuing the text in ways that are necessarily similar to those employed in the tradition from which it derives.

Even within scholarly Sanskritic circles, there have been almost as many interpretations as interpreters or schools of thought. The history of the meaning of the text, so far as we can trace it, has therefore always been that of its commentaries and interpretations, whatever their level of sophistication. Before the modern period, any systematic study of the *Gita* would always have been from within a particular commentarial tradition. This method of approaching the text has been to some extent obscured by recent attempts to present the *Gita* 'as it is'. But for all their claims, the 'fundamentalists' responsible are of course no freer of interpretative frameworks and presuppositions than their predecessors, who were usually their superiors in rigour and sophistication.

Because of its role in the history of modern Indian culture and its pivotal position in the interaction which has taken place between Indian religions and the West in the last two centuries, study of the *Gita* continues to be instructive. But there are other, perhaps more important reasons for the disinterested reader to engage with it. (I leave aside what for some may be the most compelling consideration—the question of whether it has some universally valid spiritual or religious value.) Even in translation, even cut loose from a specific tradition of commentary, the *Gita* touches on and develops in its own way many key themes from the history of Indian religions, and raises questions that are still debated. As we shall see, it is the product of a time of transition, and it attempts to reconcile diverging world views. Maybe in that—in Arjuna's predicament, if not the solution to it—lies some of the *Gita*'s appeal to our own age.

My purpose in the rest of this introduction is to provide the non-specialist reader with a brief sketch of the *Gita*'s narrative, cultural, and historical context, and to offer pointers to some of its main themes and preoccupations.

The Socio-Religious Context

The *Mahabharata*, the great epic which provides the *Gita* with its literary context, has no single author (if one discounts the mythical Vyasa). It belongs to an oral tradition that may have its origins in the eighth or ninth century BCE. Succeeding generations of reciter-poets added to, expanded on, and elaborated the basic material, which tells of a cataclysmic war between two branches of the same family and their followers. Like a snowball, the epic picked up and incorporated all the important religious, philosophical, and social changes through which it passed, often juxtaposing layers with little or no attempt at reconciliation. Nevertheless, certain themes, because they had come to preoccupy Indian religion and culture generally, began to dominate its 'poetical history': the question of what constitutes Dharma or the Law (the way things really are and therefore the way they should be), how men and women can acquire knowledge of that truth, and how they should act in relation to it.

By the time the *Gita* had been incorporated into or crystallized out of the epic (scholars are divided on which is the correct description)—perhaps in some form in the third century BCE—many of these questions had become acutely significant for what we have come to call the 'Hindu' tradition. In fact for this period that tradition is more accurately termed 'Brahminical', after the hereditary priestly class or estate which had established itself and its sacred body of knowledge, the Veda, as the arbiters of orthoprax and orthodox socio-religious conduct and values. This dominance is reflected both in the epic as we now have it and in the *Gita*. The fact that the main protagonists of the *Gita* are not brahmins at all but members of the equally hereditary warrior or ruling class should not blind us to this.

To refer to *the* Brahminical tradition is perhaps misleading, unless it is understood that by the time of the *Gita* there were a number of movements or tendencies within that tradition, not all of them obviously compatible. This led to tensions, the most significant being between those (portrayed as traditionalists) who enjoined the fulfilment of one's prescribed social and religious duties as a member of the class into which one had been born, and those who advocated renouncing that ascribed status altogether in favour of a life of homelessness and spiritual discipline.

In the Brahminical context this divergence had first come to formal light in the early *Upanishads* (a category of late Vedic texts). It was there too that the essentials of the well-known doctrine of karma and rebirth made their initial appearance. It is easy to suppose that such a doctrine developed naturally out of the ritualists' world view. The sacrifice is a mechanism for producing a result. Sacrificial action (the Sanskrit word for 'action' is *karman*), if performed correctly, produces future benefits for the sacrificer. It is therefore possible to sacrifice in order to attain a place in another world after death. The responsibility for the correct performance of the ritual lies with the brahmins, the technicians of the sacrifice, who perform the ritual on behalf of the person who desires the result. The effects of the sacrifice are, however, finite, and it has to be continually renewed. So it is not difficult to infer that the sacrificially created merit (or food), which was supposed to sustain life in the other world after death, would eventually run out. At that point one would die again, returning through various natural stages to be reborn in this world, not necessarily as a human being. The cycle is potentially endless, and from this it is a relatively short step to the conclusion that action (karma) pursued for a purpose of whatever kind results in a relatively better or worse rebirth, life after life.

At about the same time there arose the perception that since embodied existence in this world, or any other, was necessarily impermanent and subject to various ills, then even if some individuals were not suffering now they soon would be, and death was both inevitable and unpleasant. To be caught in the cycle of death and rebirth was therefore not viewed positively, as a form of immortality, but negatively as suffering, and the object was to find a way to escape it. This was not annihilationism, for against continual rebirth was postulated a goal of permanent liberation and bliss, free of physical imperfection and impermanence. The way to this new goal was first formulated in the late Vedic texts in terms of knowledge of the inner meaning of the sacrifice—what holds it together and enables it to work. Presently this was extended to everything that exists: the same principle informs and underlies all things, including the embodied or essential self. The term that was eventually settled on to designate this principle was 'Brahman'.

According to this line of thought, there was essentially no difference between the essence of the individual and Brahman, the principle underlying all things. Consequently, liberation from the cycle of death and rebirth was a matter of gnosis, for by knowing or realizing Brahman (one's own true nature) one would go to Brahman, a permanent, unchanging, and blissful state—a line of thought reiterated in the *Gita*. Purposeful sacrificial action, indeed, purposeful action of any kind could not help in this; on the contrary, because such actions were linked with a personal desire for specific results, they merely bound one more firmly to the cycle of death and rebirth. In line with this, the *Gita* itself defines Yoga as 'evenness of mind', the cultivation of an attitude of non-attachment, based on knowledge of the way things really are, which leads to 'skill in actions', that is, the ability to act without desire.[2]

According to Brahminical orthodoxy, to fulfil one's duty in one of the three higher estates[3] it was necessary to be a sacrificer, and to be a sacrificer it was necessary to be married and take a full part in the social world, the world of desire and purposeful action. Yet as we have seen, according to the Upanishadic analysis this was not conducive to liberation from rebirth and suffering. Only renunciation of the sacrificial and social world would enable the individual to approach that goal. Brahminical orthodoxy came to terms with this challenge by attempting to institutionalize renunciation as an alternative way of life that one could choose to follow after one had served one's apprenticeship as a Vedic student. This later hardened into a compulsory progression from stage to stage, with renunciation taking place only after one had fulfilled one's duties as a householder and sacrificer. When the *Gita* was formulated, however, there was clearly still an element of choice.

[2] See *Bhagavad Gita* 2.48–50.
[3] See Explanatory Note 1.41.

In the wider Indian context, neither was it a matter of a simple choice between orthodox Brahmanical renunciation and life as a ritually bound householder. Other routes, other modes of life were also available to those seeking personal liberation, chief among them the heterodox systems of Jainism and Buddhism, with their rival views of what constituted Dharma (correct behaviour in the light of the way things really are). Indeed, it was in these heterodox systems that the doctrine of karma first became fully ethicized as a moral law that was universally applicable, regardless of birth, social status, or occupation. And whether to conform to it or not was a matter for the individual alone to decide.

A cornerstone of this renunciatory morality was that deliberate injury done to other living beings was wrong and had bad karmic consequences for the person doing the injury. This is an ethical stance which provides a direct challenge to Brahminical values for, as we have seen, Brahminical society is divided into four classes or estates, and members of each estate have their own inherent dharma or duty. Persons born into a particular estate conform to the inherent duty of that estate. By doing so they help to maintain the natural order of existence and automatically accrue good results; should they deviate from their inherent duty, however, the results will be bad for them personally and for society as a whole. One of the four estates is that of the warrior or ruler, and it is a warrior's duty to fight. This is clearly antithetical to the renunciatory ideal of non-violence. From one perspective, therefore, to refrain from violence will bring bad results, but from the other, to engage in it will be similarly disastrous.

We are brought back to the *Gita*, for this is precisely Arjuna's dilemma: to conform to his inherent duty as a warrior and fight, and by doing so slaughter his enemies who are also his kinsmen, or to lay down his arms and disrupt the natural and social order. In other words, the *Gita*, through Arjuna, addresses the problem of the age: the problem of choice—of how to choose rightly.[4] One of the *Gita*'s main projects, therefore, is to

[4] Richard Gombrich has raised this question in respect of early Buddhism and Patrick Olivelle in respect of orthodox renunciation—see the select Bibliography.

reconcile or synthesize the discordant ideologies of orthodox Brahminism and renunciation—a discord that is dramatized and personified in the person of Arjuna, who finds himself caught, like Hamlet, between two world-views and two sets of values.

The resolution of this conflict is put into the mouth of Krishna, Arjuna's charioteer, comrade-in-arms, teacher, and, as revealed in the *Gita*, God omnipotent.[5] Krishna offers the distraught warrior what seems like a tier or nest of solutions. What they have in common is that they are all presented as justifications for fighting—that is to say, for acting in the world, conforming to one's inherent duty, and perpetuating the socio-religious *status quo*. From the social perspective this is deeply conservative, although what Krishna is offering in fact is a compromise. He tells Arjuna to act, but to do so without attachment to the results or fruits of his actions. In other words, he must act without desire, and that will ensure that, whatever its immediate physical consequences, the action will have no karmic repercussions for him as the apparent agent of the action. In this way it is possible to experience the soteriological benefits of renunciation without leaving society or abandoning one's inherent duty. In fact, according to Krishna, this internal renunciation is really the only way one can renounce, for the nature of material existence is such that it is impossible *not* to act.

Yet, in rejecting the way of the renouncer, Krishna is not thereby necessarily fully endorsing mainstream ritual Brahminism. His prescription to act without attachment to the fruits of action devalues the Brahminical soteriological goal of heaven, which for the orthodox is something to be attained through purposeful ritual. In other words, sacrifice as a means to personal salvation, as opposed to cosmic and social regulation, is rejected by the *Gita*. Indeed, if one is constrained to act, then the action in itself becomes soteriologically irrelevant: it is one's accompanying internal attitude that is crucial, whether one acts out of desire or out of duty. From a soteriological as opposed to a social perspective, this is subversive of orthodox values,

[5] The Krishna of later Vaishnava tradition (the tradition which considers Vishnu to be the supreme deity) is an amalgamation of the enigmatic hero-god of the *Mahabharata* and the cow-herd god of the passionately devotional movements, which nevertheless consider the *Bhagavad Gita* to be their basic text.

since it implies that, regardless of gender or class, anyone at all, simply by conforming to their class duty without attachment, can hope for salvation.

At another but related level of justification, Krishna tells Arjuna that what is permanent in the individual, the self, neither acts nor suffers the effects of action, therefore one cannot really kill or be killed. Moreover, unlike embodied beings, Krishna as God is not constrained to act; nevertheless, he does so to maintain the world, and those who are wise will follow his example. Krishna thus has a positive view of the world and the prevailing social order, for he is concerned to maintain it, and indeed intervenes by descending into the world whenever that order is threatened.[6]

Again this is an orthodox Brahminical idea somewhat recast, for the general function of sacrificial ritual is to keep the world from sliding into disorder. There is, however, another reason why Krishna should view the world positively, since by activating his lower or material nature, it is Krishna himself who has brought the universe into being, along with everything else. He is both the source and essence of all things, and the dispassionate observer of his own creation. World renunciation of the kind undertaken by 'atheistic' Jains and Buddhists, and orthodox Brahminical renouncers (with their predilection for an impersonal monism derived from speculation on the meaning of the sacrifice), seems largely incompatible with monotheism of this type. To renounce the world would be tantamount to renouncing (part of) God. Moreover, Krishna specifically states that he has created not just the material world but the social order as well, the four estates.[7]

The solution to Arjuna's problem, therefore, is to act without attachment to the results—to fight because it is his inherent duty to fight. But in a modification of this, Krishna instructs the warrior that the results of any action whatsoever should be made over to God (i.e. Krishna). And in that way one will come to God. In terms of the ideology of sacrifice, of which again this is a reformulation, this requires that both the action *and* its

[6] The *Bhagavad Gita* (4.7–8) contains the prototype of the doctrine of Vishnu's 'descents' (*avatara*).

[7] *Bhagavad Gita* 4.13

results should be offered as a sacrifice to God. In a Brahminical sacrifice the results accrue to the agent, the patron of the sacrifice, but here the results accrue to God. Whereas Brahminical ideology is anthropocentric, the *Gita* is theocentric, and in a further tier of the *Gita*'s teaching it becomes clear that the only real agent, the only real actor with regard to any and every action, *is* God. Therefore, by making over one's actions and their karmic consequences to God, one is merely conforming to the way things really are.

In the *Gita* God and the self, or the essence of the individual, are perhaps still near enough to being identical for God's agency not yet to be fatal to a sense of human effort and responsibility. Nevertheless, one thing that the spectacular and, for Arjuna, the overwhelming theophany of Chapter 11 makes clear is that God is the only true actor and humans merely the instruments of his action. *Sub specie aeternitatis* Arjuna's adversaries have already been destroyed by God: the warrior's only responsibility, therefore, is to be God's instrument in bringing about what, from this perspective, has already happened. In other words, it will come about regardless of Arjuna's intention. Acting with desire and attachment to the results of action is therefore not merely deluded but meaningless.

Where does this leave the person seeking liberation from suffering, or salvation? Krishna has already said that those who make over the results of their actions to God go to Him, and indeed that all actions should be sacrificed to Him. But beyond that, one should make such offerings with *devotion* to God: 'whoever shares in me with single-minded devotion, they are in me and I am in them.'[8] No devotee of Krishna's, regardless of social status or gender, is lost. (Again there is a change in soteriological perspective without the kind of threat to orthodox Brahminical supremacy that external, social renunciation offers.) By thinking on God, by sacrificing one's actions to Him in a spirit of ego-less non-attachment, one can earn God's grace, and through that grace one will attain supreme peace. In effect it is possible to please God by conforming to one's class duty and doing the things one has always done; yet such a strategy

[8] *Bhagavad Gita* 9.29

can only be soteriologically effective if accompanied by a radical change of attitude towards those same duty-bound actions, so that they come to be regarded not as one's own but as God's. The final chapter of the *Gita* spells this out for us, and adds a new, more personal note—one which in various forms came to dominate the relation between God and human beings in later Hindu religion, although in the context of the *Gita* as a whole it is almost an afterthought:

> Beyond that, listen to my final word, the most secret of all. You have been assuredly singled out by me, so I shall speak it for your benefit.
>
> Fix your mind on me, devote yourself to me, sacrifice to me, do homage to me, and so you shall in reality come to me. I promise you: you are dear to me.[9]

The *Gita*'s solution to Arjuna's dilemma is to formulate a compromise—a compromise reflected in the situation that obtains when Krishna finishes speaking: everything has changed (internally) and everything remains the same (externally). In terms of the epic narrative, Arjuna can now pick up his bow again and the battle can start.

The Narrative Context

At the core of the *Mahabharata* is the story of the struggle for the kingdom of Bharata (roughly northern India), the world of the original audience for the poem. (Modern India is known by the same name.) The contending parties are cousins, the children of two royal brothers. The elder of the two brothers, Dhritarashtra, has been born blind, so the younger one, Pandu, rules in his stead. Pandu dies, leaving five young sons—Yudhishthira, Bhima, and Arjuna from one wife, and Nakula and Sahadeva from another. Collectively, they are known as the Pandavas, 'descendants of Pandu'. Dhritarashtra, who in spite of his blindness has now become king, is the father of a hundred sons, known as the Kauravas, 'descendants of Kuru'.[10] The eldest of the Kauravas is Duryodhana.

[9] *Bhagavad Gita* 18.64–65

[10] Kuru is in fact a common ancestor of both sets of cousins, as is (the man) Bharata, '(Descendant of) Bharata' being another common epithet.

A simmering rivalry between the cousins, the Pandavas and Kauravas, over the legitimate succession threatens to boil into war. In an attempt to avert this the blind Dhritarashtra divides the kingdom in two, one part to be ruled by Duryodhana, the other by Yudishthira. But this only postpones hostilities, and eventually Duryodhana challenges the virtuous Yudhishthira to a game of dice. Yudhishthira loses everything—not just his kingdom, but his brothers, himself, and their joint wife, Draupadi. The Kauravas brutally humiliate Draupadi, ensuring that the war, when it comes, will be a vengeful one. In what is literally a last throw of the dice, Yudhishthira gambles again. This time the losers are to be exiled to the forest for twelve years and to spend a thirteenth year incognito. Only if these conditions are met in full can they then legitimately return and reclaim their kingdom. Yudhishthira loses again and the Pandavas go into exile.

After many adventures and, in the *Mahabharata* as we have it, much religious teaching, the Pandavas return after thirteen years to claim what is theirs. Duryodhana, however, refuses to give it up. War can now no longer be averted.

Each side assembles its allies. Among them is Krishna, the king of Dvaraka, who has links with both parties. He therefore gives his armies to fight on the Kaurava side, and goes himself to assist the Pandavas as Arjuna's charioteer. And this is where the *Bhagavad Gita* begins. The old blind king, Dhritarashtra, has asked his bard, Sanjaya, to report the events of the war to him, and the *Gita* constitutes part of his narrative.

The two armies are facing each other. Arjuna, the great warrior, the great archer, is in his chariot, driven by Krishna, and the battle is about to start. Suddenly Arjuna is overcome by apparently disabling moral scruples: how can it be right to kill his kinsmen? He avows his intention not to fight and sinks disconsolately into his chariot. This is totally unexpected and all the more shocking because of Arjuna's heroic martial status. Real time, as is common enough in the epic, then comes to a halt while Krishna addresses the reluctant warrior.

If the way Arjuna is portrayed in the *Gita* is unexpected in the context of the rest of the *Mahabharata*, the treatment of Krishna is astonishing. More than an ally or even a teacher (although he is both those), he reveals himself as the universal God. Certainly he has previously demonstrated some miraculous powers, but this revelation is of a different order. Indeed, so overwhelming is it that Arjuna finds it not only too much to bear but also apparently too much to remember. What does not fade, however, is the warrior's renewed determination to fight, inspired by what Krishna has shown and taught him.

The *Bhagavad Gita* finishes here, at the moment in the epic when total war begins. After eighteen days of carnage, the Pandavas emerge victorious and Yudhishthira becomes king. Later, in his ambiguous hero mould, Krishna is killed in a hunting accident in the forest. The Pandava brothers hand on their hard-won kingdom and set off for the Himalayas in search of the king of the gods' heaven, but only Yudhishthira, the embodiment of Dharma, reaches it alive. The others, including Arjuna, the troubled warrior of the *Gita*, perish on the way.

NOTE ON THE TEXT AND TRANSLATION

The *Bhagavad Gita* as we have it now is the same text on which the great Vedantin teacher Shankara wrote a commentary around the beginning of the eighth century CE. Indeed the critical edition, published in India in 1947, follows (with some minor exceptions) Shankara's version. Whatever ultimate reality he accorded to a personal god, Shankara uncontroversially regarded the *Gita* as the teaching of the Lord Himself, as recorded by Vyasa. In fact the *Gita* seems to have enjoyed this elevated status within the Vedanta system from relatively soon after its original appearance, although Shankara's is the earliest surviving commentary.

Technically the *Gita* does not belong to the uncreated, beginningless and self-authenticating or revealed category of Vedic literature (the Veda itself). Rather it belongs to that tradition (literally, 'what has been remembered') which implicitly derives its authority from the Veda. But by Vaishnavas[1] in particular, and increasingly by most Hindus, the *Gita* came to be regarded as having the same religious authority as a revealed text—that is to say, to all intents and purposes it was accorded an autonomous authority worthy of commentarial exegesis.

This is not the place to attempt a survey of the various commentaries on the *Gita*; the interested reader is referred to the works cited in the Bibliography. The question of the *Gita*'s 'real' meaning does, however, raise additional problems for the translator, in so far as all translation inevitably involves interpretation, and any translation which seeks, as this one does, to render most of the Sanskrit technical terminology into English, interprets more than others. Where the Sanskrit original may remain open to a variety of readings, the English translation fixes on one, not arbitrarily so in the eyes of the translator, but nevertheless with a greater or lesser degree of compromise. It

[1] Vaishnavas are those Hindus who consider Vishnu to be the supreme God. The *Bhagavad Gita*'s Krishna is assumed by them to be Vishnu.

follows from this that, just as there can be no definitive performance of a Shakespeare play, so there can be no definitive translation of a text such as the *Gita*—which is one reason why so many have been attempted.

SELECT BIBLIOGRAPHY

The standard text of the *Bhagavad Gita* in Sanskrit, and the one used for this translation, is that prepared for the critical edition of the *Mahabharata* edited by S. K. Belvalkar: *Mahābhārata*, volume 7, *Bhīṣmaparvan* (Poona: Bhandarkar Oriental Research Institute, 1947), pp. 114–88.

There have been many translations of the *Gita* into English. As possible starting-points for readers wishing to further their study of the text, I mention here just three of the more widely available scholarly versions:

Franklin Edgerton, *The Bhagavad Gītā, translated and interpreted* (2 volumes, Harvard Oriental Series, nos 38 and 39, Cambridge, Massachusetts: Harvard University Press, 1944); reprinted in 1 volume, 1972.

R. C. Zaehner, *The Bhagavad-Gītā, with a commentary based on the original sources* (Oxford University Press, 1969).

J. A. B. van Buitenen, *The Bhagavadgītā in the Mahābhārata*, text and translation (University of Chicago Press, 1981).

All these (with the exception of the paperback reprint of Edgerton's translation) contain the transliterated Sanskrit text. Franklin Edgerton's translation is the most literal and he includes a useful series of interpretative essays. R. C. Zaehner's version is scholarly and contains much commentarial material not otherwise available in English, although his own (Christian) religious position sometimes intrudes. J. A. B. van Buitenen's edition has an interesting introductory essay and, as its title suggests, places the *Gita* in its epic context by translating the whole of the portion of the *Mahabharata* in which it is embedded (a book known as the *Bhagavadgītāparvan*).

Shelves, if not libraries of books and articles have been written about or around the *Gita* in English alone. Two books, one dealing with some of the major classical commentaries, the other with modern interpretations and interpreters, may serve as introductions to this mountain of material:

Arvind Sharma, *The Hindu Gītā: Ancient and Classical Interpretations of the Bhagavadgītā* (London: Duckworth, 1986).
Eric J. Sharpe, *The Universal Gītā: Western Images of the Bhagavadgītā* (London: Duckworth, 1985).

For the reader wishing to place the *Gita* in its wider cultural and historical context, some more general studies of Hinduism may be recommended, for instance:

A. L. Basham, *The Wonder that was India* (London: Sidgwick and Jackson, 1967)
Madeleine Biardeau, *Hinduism: The Anthropology of a Civilization*, translated from the French by Richard Nice (Delhi: Oxford University Press, 1989).
J. L. Brockington, *The Sacred Thread: Hinduism in its Continuity and Diversity* (Edinburgh University Press, 1981).
Thomas J. Hopkins, *The Hindu Religious Tradition* (Belmont, Cal.: Dickenson, 1971).
Klaus K. Klostermaier, *A Survey of Hinduism* (Albany, New York: State University of New York Press, 1989).

A more specialized work, which in its lengthy introduction gives the background to orthodox renunciation, is Patrick Olivelle's *Saṃnyāsa Upaniṣads: Hindu Scriptures on Asceticism and Renunciation* (New York: Oxford University Press, 1992). And for a readable but scholarly study of, among other things, the social factors conducive to renunciatory movements in ancient India and the problem of choice (albeit in the context of Buddhism), there is Richard Gombrich's *Theravāda Buddhism: A Social History from Ancient Benares to Modern Colombo* (London: Routledge and Kegan Paul, 1988). I owe a number of the ideas in my introduction to these works.

NOTE ON METRE

In its original form the *Bhagavad Gita* is in unrhymed Sanskrit verse. Most individual verses have thirty-two syllables, a metre known as *shloka*. Occasionally (notably in Chapter 11) another metre, the *trishtubh* is used, consisting of verses of forty-four syllables each. Within these basic forms there are various prescribed patterns of long and short syllables. No attempt has been made to reproduce or mirror these metres in the translation, which is in prose. The verses in *trishtubh* have, however, been printed in smaller type to indicate where a change in metre takes place. The type size is purely conventional and should not be taken in itself to imply anything about the importance or otherwise of the verses so printed. If anything, the *trishtubh* metre gives an impression of greater weight in the original.

NOTE ON TYPOGRAPHY IN CHAPTER 1

In Chapter 1, to ease the non-specialist reader through the thicket of unfamiliar and, in the context of the rest of the *Gita*, mostly irrelevant characters, the names of the *Kauravas* and their allies are printed in italics, those of the **Pandavas** and their allies in bold. (On Kauravas and Pandavas, and some of the major *dramatis personae*, see 'The Narrative Context' in the Introduction.) This practice is dispensed with for the remaining chapters, where most names or epithets refer in an obvious way to either Krishna or Arjuna.

THE BHAGAVAD GITA

CHAPTER 1

Dhritarashtra said:

(1) In the Field of the Law,* the Kurus' Field, when my men and the **Pandava** men had come together so eager to fight, what did they do, *Sanjaya*?*

Sanjaya said:

(2) Once he had seen the **Pandava** army drawn up for battle, *King Duryodhana* approached the teacher, *Drona*, and said:

(3) 'Master, behold this mighty army of **Pandu**'s sons drawn up by your wise student, **Dhrishtadyumna**, **Drupada**'s son.

(4) 'Here are champions, great archers, equals in battle of **Bhima** and **Arjuna**: **Yuyudhana**, **Virata**, and the great warrior **Drupada**,

(5) '**Dhrishtaketu**, **Chekitana**, and the dynamic king of the **Kashis**, **Purujit**, **Kuntibhoja**, and **Shaibya**, a bull among men,

(6) 'Bold **Yudhamanyu** and valiant **Uttamaujas**, **Subhadra**'s son, and the sons of **Draupadi**, great warriors to a man.

(7) 'But now, greatest of brahmins, mark our chief men, the commanders of my army—for you I shall list them by name:

(8) 'Yourself, *Bhishma*, *Karna*, and *Kripa*, victorious in battle, *Ashvatthaman*, *Vikarna*, as well as *Somadatta*'s son,

(9) 'And many other champions who have given up their lives to my cause, all battle-hardened combatants, armed to the teeth.

(10) 'Their force, protected by **Bhima**, is no match for ours; but ours is good enough for them—it is protected by *Bhishma*.*

(11) 'So all of you, waiting now in your proper places—you must guard *Bhishma* at every turn!'

(12) Then the elder of the Kurus, the Grandfather, *Bhishma*, roared a great lion's roar, and blew vigorously on his conch, bringing joy to *Duryodhana*.

(13) Thereupon conches, kettledrums, cymbals, drums, and horns suddenly blared out in a tumult of sound.

(14) And so, as they stood in a great chariot yoked with white horses, **Krishna** and **Arjuna** blew their divine conches—

(15) **Krishna** the conch Panchajanya, **Arjuna** Devadatta, and wolf-belly **Bhima**, so terrible in action, blew the great conch Paundra.

(16) **Yudhishthira**, son of Kunti and king, blew Anantavijaya, **Nakula** and **Sahadeva** blew Sughosha and Manipushpaka.

(17) And the king of the **Kashis**, supreme bowman, **Shikhandin** the great warrior, **Dhrishtadyumna** and **Virata**, and **Satyaki** the unconquered,

(18) **Drupada** and the **sons of Draupadi**, O King of the Earth, and the great-armed **son of Subhadra**, in unison blew their separate conches.

(19) That sound lacerated the hearts of *Dhritarashtra's sons*—an uproar that thundered from heaven to earth.

(20) Then the ape-bannered **Pandava, Arjuna**, seeing *Dhritarashtra*'s host drawn up for battle, raised his bow aloft as the clash of arms was coming on,

(21) And, O King of the Earth, said to **Krishna**: 'Achyuta, draw up my chariot between the two armies

(22) 'That I may look on these men, at the ready, eager for battle, with whom I must engage in this great enterprise of war.

(23) 'I would see those assembled here, straining to fight, eager to serve in battle *Duryodhana*, *Dhritarashtra*'s evil-minded son.'

(24) Addressed thus by **Arjuna**, O Bharata, **Krishna** halted the great chariot between the two armies,

(25) In front of *Bhishma*, and *Drona*, and all the lords of the earth, and said: 'Look, Partha, these are the Kurus, all of them together.'

(26) There **Arjuna** saw, standing their ground, fathers, grandfathers, teachers, maternal uncles, brothers, sons, grandsons, friends,

(27) Fathers-in-law, and companions in both armies. And looking at all these kinsmen so arrayed, **Arjuna**, the son of Kunti,

(28) Was overcome by deep compassion; and in despair he said: 'Krishna, when I see these my own people eager to fight, on the brink,

(29) 'My limbs grow heavy, and my mouth is parched, my body trembles and my hair bristles,

(30) 'My bow, Gandiva, falls from my hand, my skin's on fire, I can no longer stand—my mind is reeling,

(31) 'I see evil omens, Krishna: nothing good can come from slaughtering one's own family in battle—I foresee it!

(32) 'I have no desire for victory, Krishna, or kingship, or pleasures. What should we do with kingship, Govinda? What are pleasures to us? What is life?

(33) 'The men for whose sake we desire kingship, enjoyment, and pleasures are precisely those drawn up for this battle, having abandoned their lives and riches.

(34) 'Teachers, fathers, sons, as well as grandfathers, maternal uncles, fathers-in-law, grandsons, brothers-in-law, and kinsmen—

(35) 'I have no desire to kill them, Madhusudana, though they are killers themselves—no, not for the lordship of the three worlds,* let alone the earth!

(36) 'Where is the joy for us, Janardana, in destroying *Dhritarashtra*'s people? Having killed these murderers, evil would attach itself to us.

(37) 'It follows, therefore, that we are not required to kill the sons of *Dhritarashtra*—they are our own kinsmen,* and having killed our own people, how could we be happy, Madhava?

(38) 'And even if, because their minds are overwhelmed by greed, *they* cannot see the evil incurred by destroying one's own family, and the degradation involved in the betrayal of a friend,

(39) 'How can *we* be so ignorant as not to recoil from this wrong? The evil incurred by destroying one's own family is plain to see, Janardana.

(40) 'With the destruction of family the eternal family laws are lost; when the law is destroyed, lawlessness overpowers the entire family.

(41) 'Krishna, because of overpowering lawlessness, the women of the family are corrupted; when women are corrupted, Varshneya, there is intermingling of the four estates.*

(42) 'And intermingling leads to hell for the family-destroyers *and* the family, for their ancestors, robbed of their rice-ball and water offerings, fall back.*

(43) 'Through these evils of the family-destroyers, which cause intermingling of the four estates, caste laws and the eternal family laws are obliterated.

(44) 'For men whose family laws have been obliterated we have heard that a place in hell is certain, Janardana.

(45) 'Oh, ignominy! We are about to perpetrate a great evil—out of sheer greed for kingdoms and pleasures, we are prepared to kill our own people.

(46) 'It would be better for me if *Dhritarashtra*'s armed men were to kill me in battle, unresisting and unarmed.'

(47) Having spoken this on the field of conflict, Arjuna sank down into the chariot, letting slip his bow and arrow, his mind distracted with grief.

CHAPTER 2

Sanjaya said:

(1) Then, Krishna, the destroyer of the demon Madhu, spoke these words to the dejected Arjuna, who, eyes blurred and brimming with tears, was so overcome by pity:

The Lord said:

(2) Arjuna, where do you get this weakness from at a moment of crisis? A noble should not experience this. It does not lead to heaven, it leads to disgrace.

(3) No impotence, Partha, it does not become you. Abandon this base, inner weakness. Get up, Incinerator of the Foe!

Arjuna said:

(4) Destroyer of Madhu, destroyer of the enemy, how can I shoot arrows at Bhishma and Drona in battle when they should be honoured?

(5) Better to eat begged food among common people than to kill such worthy teachers. For having killed my teachers, who desire legitimate worldly ends, I should be consuming food smeared with blood.

(6) And we do not know which is better for us—that we should overcome Dhritarashtra's men, standing there before us, or that they should overcome us. For if we were to kill them, we should have no desire to go on living.

(7) My inner being is disabled by that vice of dejection. My mind is bewildered as to what is right. I ask you, which would be better? Tell me for certain. I am your student, I have come to you for help. Instruct me!

(8) Though I were to obtain a prosperous, unrivalled kingdom on earth, and even mastery over the gods, I cannot imagine what could dispel my grief, which withers the senses.

Sanjaya said:

(9) And having spoken thus to Krishna, to Govinda, having said 'I will not fight!' Arjuna, the Incinerator of the Foe, fell silent.

(10) O Dhritarashtra, between the two armies, Krishna, with the shadow of a smile, spoke these words to that dejected man:

The Lord said:

(11) You utter wise *words*, yet you have been mourning those who should not be mourned; the truly wise do not grieve for the living or the dead.

(12) There never was a time when I was not, or you, or these rulers of men. Nor will there ever be a time when we shall cease to be, all of us hereafter.

(13) Just as within this body the embodied self passes through childhood, youth, and old age, so it passes to another body. The wise man is not bewildered by this.

(14) But contacts with matter, Son of Kunti, give rise to cold and heat, pleasure and pain. They come and go, Bharata; they are impermanent and you should endure them.

(15) For these things, Bull among men, do not perturb that wise man for whom pleasure and pain are the same; he is ready for immortality.

(16) For the non-existent there is no coming into existence, for the existent there is no lapsing into non-existence; the division between them is observed by those who see the underlying nature of things.

(17) But know that that on which all this is stretched is indestructible. No one can destroy this imperishable one.

(18) It is just these *bodies* of the indestructible, immeasurable, and eternal embodied self that are characterized as coming to an end—therefore fight, Bharata!

(19) Anyone who believes this a killer, and anyone who thinks this killed, they do not understand: it does not kill, it is not killed

(20) It is not born, it never dies; being, it will never again cease to be. It is unborn, invariable, eternal, primeval. It is not killed when the body is killed.

(21) Partha, how can that man who knows it to be indestructible, invariable, unborn, and imperishable bring about the death of anyone? Whom does he kill?

(22) Just as a man casting off worn-out clothes takes up others that are new, so the embodied self, casting off its worn-out bodies, goes to other, new ones.

(23) Blades do not pierce it, fire does not burn it, waters do not wet it, and the wind does not parch it.

(24) It cannot be pierced, it cannot be burned, it cannot be wetted, it cannot be parched. It is invariable, everywhere, fixed, immovable, eternal.

(25) It is said to be imperceptible, unthinkable, and immutable; knowing it to be so, you should not therefore grieve.

(26) And even if you believe that it is regularly born and regularly dead, you should not grieve for it, Great Arm.

(27) Death is inevitable for those who are born; for those who are dead birth is just as certain. Therefore you must not grieve for what is ineluctable.

(28) Bharata, beings have imperceptible beginnings; the interim is clear; their ends are again indistinct. What is there to lament in this?

(29) Quite exceptionally does anyone see it, and quite exceptionally does anyone speak of it; it is quite exceptional for anyone to hear of it, but even when they have heard of it, no one in fact knows it.

(30) Bharata, this embodied self in the body of everyone is eternally unkillable. Therefore you must not grieve for any beings at all.

(31) Recognizing your inherent duty, you must not shrink from it. For there is nothing better for a warrior than a duty-bound war.

(32) It is a door to heaven, opened fortuitously. Fortunate are the warriors, Partha, who are presented with such a war.

(33) But if, careless of your inherent duty and renown, you will not undertake this duty-bound conflict, you shall transgress.

(34) Moreover, people will recount your limitless disgrace—and disgrace is worse than death for the man who has once been honoured.

(35) The great warriors will suppose that you withdrew from the battle out of fear. And you will fade from their high regard into insignificance.

(36) Then your enemies will say many things that would be better unsaid, slighting your strength—and what could be more painful than that?

(37) You will either be killed and attain heaven, or conquer and enjoy the earth. So rise, Son of Kunti, determined to fight.

(38) Making yourself indifferent to pleasure and pain, gain and loss, victory and defeat, commit yourself to battle. And in that way you shall not transgress.

(39) You have received this intelligence according to Sankhya theory,* now hear it as it applies to practice. Disciplined with such intelligence, Partha, you shall throw off the bondage of action.

(40) In this there is no wasted effort, no reverse; just a little of this truth saves from great danger.

(41) Son of the Kurus, in this the resolute intelligence is one, the intellects of the irresolute are without limit and many-branched.

(42) Partha, that florid speech the uninspired utter, addicted to the words of the Veda,* claiming that there is nothing else,

(43) Their nature desire, their aim heaven—that speech which produces rebirth as the fruit of action, and which is dense with specific ritual acts aimed at the attainment of enjoyment and power,

(44) Robs those addicted to enjoyment and power of their minds. For them no resolute intelligence is established in concentration.

(45) The Vedas' sphere of activity is the three constituents of material nature.* Arjuna, be free from the three constituents, free from duality, forever grounded in purity, beyond getting and keeping, possessed of the self.

(46) For the brahmin who knows, there is no more purpose in all the Vedas than in a water-tank surrounded by a flood.

(47) You are qualified simply with regard to action, never with regard to its results. You must be neither motivated by the results of action nor attached to inaction.

withdrawal of the senses: — The TORTOISE

(48) Grounded in yogic discipline, and having abandoned attachment, undertake actions, Dhananjaya, evenly disposed as to their success or failure. Yoga is defined as evenness of mind.

(49) For action in itself is inferior by far to the discipline of intelligence, Dhananjaya. You must seek refuge in intelligence. Those motivated by results are wretched.

(50) The man disciplined in intelligence renounces in this world the results of both good and evil actions. Therefore commit yourself to yogic discipline; yogic discipline is skill in actions.

(51) For, having abandoned the result produced from action, those who understand, who are disciplined in intelligence, are freed from the bondage of rebirth and achieve a state without disease.

(52) When your intelligence emerges from the thicket of delusion, then you will become disenchanted with what is to be heard and has been heard in the Veda.

(53) When, turned away from the Veda, your intelligence stands motionless, immovable in concentration, then you will attain yogic discipline.

Arjuna said:

(54) O Keshava, how do you describe that man whose mentality is stable, whose concentration is fixed? What should the man whose thought is settled say? How should he sit? How should he walk?

The Lord said:

(55) Partha, when he abandons every desire lodged in the mind, by himself content within the self, then he is called a man of stable mentality.

(56) He is called a holy man, settled in thought, whose mind is not disturbed in the midst of sorrows, who has lost the desire for pleasures, whose passion, fear, and anger have disappeared.

(57) His mentality is stabilized who feels no desire for anything, for getting this or that good or evil, and who neither rejoices in nor loathes anything.

(58) When this man, like a tortoise retracting its limbs, entirely withdraws his senses from the objects of sense, his mentality is stabilized.

(59) For the embodied being who does not feed on them the objects of sense disappear, except flavour; flavour fades too for the one who has seen the highest.

(60) Son of Kunti, even for the man of discernment who strives, the harassing senses forcibly seize the mind.

(61) Restraining all the senses, one should sit, yogically disciplined, focused on me; for if one's senses are under control one's mentality is grounded.

(62) When a man meditates on the objects of sense he becomes attached to them; from attachment desire is born, from desire anger.

(63) Out of anger confusion arises, through confusion memory wanders, from loss of memory the intelligence is destroyed; from the destruction of intelligence a man is lost.

(64) But engaging the objects of sense with his senses separated from desire and loathing, and subject to the will of the self, a man who is self-controlled attains calmness.

(65) In calm all his miseries are ended, for the intelligence of the man whose mind is calm is immediately stabilized.

(66) The undisciplined man has no intelligence, and no capacity to produce anything, and one who has no capacity is without serenity. And how can there be happiness for the man who lacks serenity?

(67) For a mind conforming to the wandering senses carries away one's insight, as the wind a ship on the water.

(68) Therefore, Great Arm, whoever has entirely withheld the senses from the objects of sense has stabilized his insight.

(69) When it is night for all creatures, the man who restrains himself is awake; when creatures are awake, it is night for the perceptive seer.

(70) Just as waters enter the sea, which is forever being filled although its depths are unmoving, so the man whom all desires enter in the same way attains peace—but not the desirer of desires.

(71) The man who, having abandoned all desires, lives free from longing, unpossessive and unegoistical, approaches peace.

(72) This, Partha, is the Brahman state; having attained it, one is not deluded; fixed in it, even at the moment of death one reaches the nirvana of Brahman.*

CHAPTER 3

Arjuna said:

(1) Krishna, if it is your belief that the way of intelligence is superior to action, then why do you enjoin me, Keshava, to this terrible undertaking?

(2) With such equivocal words you seem to confuse my intelligence. Describe clearly an unambiguous way through which I may attain what is best.

The Lord said:

(3) Blameless one, I have taught of old that in this world two ways are open: the discipline of knowledge for Sankhya theorists,* and the discipline of action for yogins.

(4) A man does not attain freedom from the results of action by abstaining from actions, and he does not approach perfection simply by renunciation.

(5) For no one ever, even for a moment, exists without acting; everyone, regardless of their will, is made to perform actions by the constituents which originate from material nature.*

(6) The man who, having restrained his action organs, then sits with his mind preoccupied with sense objects, is called a self-deluding hypocrite.

(7) But the man who, controlling his senses with his mind, undertakes through his action organs the discipline of action without attachment, distinguishes himself, Arjuna.

(8) You should perform enjoined action, for action is better than non-action; even the minimum of bodily subsistence would be impossible without action.

(9) The entire world is bound by actions; the only exception is action undertaken for sacrificial purposes. Therefore, Son of Kunti, free from attachment, you should perform that kind of action.

(10) When he created creatures in the beginning, along with the sacrifice, Prajapati* said: 'May you be fruitful by

this sacrifice, let this be the cow which produces all you desire.

(11) 'You should nourish the gods with this so that the gods may nourish you; nourishing each other, you shall achieve the highest good.

(12) 'For nourished by the sacrifice, the gods will give you the pleasures you desire. The man who enjoys these gifts without repaying them is no more than a thief.'

(13) The virtuous who eat the remainder of the sacrifice are released from all faults; the wicked who cook for the sake of themselves consume impurity.

(14) Beings exist through food, the origin of food is rain, rain comes from sacrifice, sacrifice derives from action.

(15) Know that action originates from Brahman—Brahman whose source is the imperishable. Therefore all-pervading Brahman is eternally established in the sacrifice.*

(16) Whoever in this world does not turn the wheel thus set in motion, Partha, lives in vain, making a pleasure garden of his senses, intent upon evil.

(17) But it is clear that, for the man who delights in the self, and is satisfied with the self, and fulfilled only in the self, there is nothing that has to be done.*

(18) For him there is no significance whatsoever in what has been done or has not been done in this world, and he has no kind of dependence at all on any being.

(19) Therefore, without attachment, always do whatever action has to be done; for it is through acting without attachment that a man attains the highest.

(20) Indeed, it was by action alone that King Janaka* and others attained perfection. Looking only to what maintains the world, you too must act.

(21) Whatever the superior man does, so do the rest; whatever standard he sets, the world follows it.

(22) Partha, as for me there is nothing whatever that has to be done in the three worlds;* there is nothing unaccomplished to be accomplished. Yet I still engage in action.

(23) For were I not to engage tirelessly in action, humans everywhere would follow in my wake, Partha.

(24) If I did not engage in action, these worlds would fall into ruin; I should be the instrument of anarchy; I should destroy these creatures.

(25) Just as the ignorant act out of attachment to action, Bharata, so the wise should also act, but without attachment, intent upon maintaining the world.

(26) The wise man should not disturb the minds of those ignorant people who are attached to action; acting in a disciplined manner himself, he should encourage involvement in all actions.

(27) In every case, actions are performed by the constituents of material nature; although the man who is deluded by egotism thinks to himself, '*I* am the actor.'

(28) But he who knows the principle underlying the division of constituents and actions, understanding that it is constituents that are acting on constituents, is not attached, Great Arm.

(29) The person whose knowledge is comprehensive should not agitate those dullards whose knowledge is not so great—those who are deluded by the constituents of material nature and attached to the actions of the constituents.

(30) Giving up all actions to me, with your mind on what relates to the self, desireless and not possessive, fight! Your fever is past.

(31) Faithful, uncontentious men, who constantly practise this doctrine of mine, are also released from the results of action.

(32) But you should know that those who object to this, who do not follow my doctrine, and who are blind to all knowledge, are mindless and lost.

(33) Even the one who knows acts in accordance with his own material nature. Creatures conform to material nature—what good will repression do?

(34) In the case of a sense, desire and aversion adhere to the object of that sense; you should not fall into the power of those two, for they will block your path.

(35) It is better to practise your own inherent duty deficiently than another's duty well. It is better to die

conforming to your own duty; the duty of others invites danger.

Arjuna said:

(36) So what is it that impels a man to do evil, Varshneya, even unwillingly, as though compelled to it by force?

The Lord said:

(37) It is desire, it is anger, produced from the constituent of passion, all-consuming, all-injuring; know that that is the enemy here.

(38) As a fire is covered by smoke and a mirror by dust; as an embryo is covered by a sac, this world is enveloped by that.

(39) By this perpetual enemy of the wise, by this insatiable fire in the form of desire, knowledge is obscured, Son of Kunti.

(40) It is said that the senses, the mind, and the intelligence are its locality; having obscured a man's knowledge with these, it deludes the embodied self.

(41) Therefore, having first restrained the senses, Bull of the Bharatas, strike down this evil thing, the destroyer of insight and knowledge.

(42) They say that the senses are great; the mind is greater than the senses. Yet greater than the mind is the intelligence; but he* is that which is still greater than the intelligence.

(43) So, Great Arm, having learned what is higher than the intelligence, and having strengthened yourself through the self, kill that enemy in the shape of desire, so difficult to pin down.

CHAPTER 4

The Lord said:

(1) I taught this eternal way to Vivasvat; Vivasvat showed it to Manu; Manu told it to Ikshvaku.*

(2) And it was this way, passed on from teacher to teacher in an unbroken line, that the royal seers knew. Over a long period of time here on earth that track was obliterated, Incinerator of the Foe.

(3) It is this very same ancient way that I have shown you now, for you are devoted, and my friend, and this is the most secret teaching.

Arjuna said:

(4) You were born recently, Vivasvat was born a long time ago, so what should I understand by the saying that you taught it in the beginning?

The Lord said:

(5) I have passed through many births, and so have you, Arjuna. I know them all, you do not, Incinerator of the Foe.

(6) Although I am unborn and have a self that is eternal, although I am lord of beings, by controlling my own material nature I come into being by means of my own incomprehensible power.

(7) Whenever there is a falling away from the true law and an upsurge of unlawfulness, then, Bharata, I emit myself.

(8) I come into being age after age, to protect the virtuous and to destroy evil-doers, to establish a firm basis for the true law.

(9) Whoever knows my divine birth and action as they really are is not born again on leaving the body. He comes to me, Arjuna.

(10) There are many, free of passion, fear, and anger, at one with me, taking refuge in me, who, refined in the heat of knowledge, have come to my state of being.

(11) I favour them according to the manner in which they approach me. Men, Partha, universally follow my path.

(12) Desiring the attainment that comes from ritual acts, men here sacrifice to the gods; for in the human world the attainment born of sacrificial action comes quickly.

(13) The four estates* were created by me, divided according to constituents and actions. Although I alone am the one who did this, know that I am an eternal non-actor.

(14) Actions do not taint me. I have no desire for the results of action. Whoever understands that I am like this is not bound by actions.

(15) Men of old who desired release knew this and acted. Therefore you should act as they once acted.

(16) What is action, what is non-action? Even inspired seers are confused about this. Such action I shall explain to you, and understanding it you shall be freed from evil.

(17) You should know what constitutes action, wrong action, and non-action. The way of action runs deep.

(18) He who sees action in non-action, non-action in action, is wise among men; performing all actions he is disciplined.

(19) The wise call him a man of learning whose every activity is free from desire and specific intention; his actions are consumed in the fire of knowledge.

(20) That man who depends upon nothing, who has given up attachment to the results of action, is perpetually satisfied, and even though engaged in action he does nothing whatsoever.

(21) Acting for the body alone, without expectation, having abandoned possessions, restrained in thought and self, he incurs no defilement.

(22) Content with what comes by chance, having gone beyond dualities, free from envy, the same in success and in failure, even when he has acted he is not bound.

(23) For the man who is rid of attachment, who has attained release, whose thought is anchored in knowledge, action is sacrificial and melts entirely away.

(24) The offering is Brahman, the oblation is Brahman, poured by Brahman into the fire that is Brahman. Brahman is to be attained by that man who concentrates intensely on the action that is Brahman.*

(25) Some skilled performers concentrate on sacrifice to one of the deities; some offer sacrifice through the sacrifice itself into the fire of Brahman;

(26) Others offer the senses (such as hearing) into the fires of restraint; others again offer the objects of the senses (such as sound) into the fires of the senses;

(27) Some offer all actions of sense and breath into the fire of the discipline of self-restraint, kindled by knowledge.

(28) Similarly there are others, sacrificers with material substance, with bodily mortification, with spiritual exercise, with Vedic study and knowledge—ascetics with uncompromising vows.

(29) And again, those whose object is breath-control offer the inhaled into the exhaled breath, and the exhaled into the inhaled, restricting their passage.

(30) Others, who have put limits on their consumption of food, offer their inhalation into their inhalation. All these, who know what sacrifice is, have their imperfections obliterated by sacrifice.

(31) Those who eat the immortality-conferring remnants of the sacrifice go to primeval Brahman. Best of Kurus, this world, let alone the other, is not for non-sacrificers.

(32) Thus many kinds of sacrifice are stretched out in the mouth of Brahman. Remember that they are all born of action; knowing that, you will be liberated.

(33) Incinerator of the Foe, the sacrifice of knowledge is better than the sacrifice of material substance. There is no action whatsoever, Partha, which is not concluded in knowledge.

(34) Know this: through your submission, through the questions you ask, through your service, those who have knowledge, who see things as they are, will teach you knowledge.

(35) And having it, you will never be bewildered in such a way again, Pandava. Through it you shall see all creatures in yourself, and then in me.

(36) Even if you are the very worst of all transgressors, with the boat of knowledge you shall plot a safe course through all crookedness.

(37) As a lighted fire reduces kindling to ash, in the same way, Arjuna, the fire of knowledge incinerates all actions.

(38) Nothing on earth has the purificatory power of knowledge; eventually, the man who has perfected his disciplined practice discovers it in himself.

(39) Restraining his senses, the man of faith who is devoted to knowledge attains it. And having attained knowledge, he rapidly achieves supreme peace.

(40) The faithless and ignorant man, whose nature it is to doubt, perishes. Not this world, nor the one beyond, nor happiness exists for the doubter.

(41) But the self-possessed man, Dhananjaya, who has renounced action through discipline, and cut through doubt with knowledge, is not bound by actions.

(42) Therefore, having severed with the blade of knowledge this doubt of yours, which stems from ignorance and is fixed in the heart, act with discipline, Bharata—arise!

CHAPTER 5

Arjuna said:

(1) Krishna, you approve the renunciation of actions, and then again the practice of yogic discipline. Tell me unambiguously, which is the better of these two?

The Lord said:

(2) Both renunciation and the practice of yogic action lead to ultimate bliss, but, of the two, the practice of yogic action is superior to the renunciation of action.

(3) Great Arm, the man who neither desires nor hates is considered a perpetual renouncer; free from duality, he is easily liberated.

(4) Fools hold that the way of Sankhya* and the practice of yogic action are different, but not those who know. Through either one of them, carried out properly, one attains the reward of both.

(5) The state achieved by Sankhyas is also achieved by yogic actors; whoever sees the ways of Sankhya and yogic action as one truly sees.

(6) But renunciation, Great Arm, is hard to attain without yogic practice; the sage disciplined in yogic practice swiftly reaches Brahman.

(7) Even when he is acting, the man who is disciplined in yogic practice, whose self is pure, whose self and senses are controlled, whose self is the self of all beings, is not defiled.

(8–9) The disciplined man, who knows the underlying principle of reality, thinks: 'I really don't do anything at all,' certain that whether seeing, hearing, touching, smelling, eating, walking, sleeping, breathing, talking, excreting, grasping, opening or shutting the eyes, it is merely the senses acting on the objects of sense.

(10) The man who acts, having rendered his actions to Brahman and abandoned attachment, is untainted by evil, in the same way that a lotus leaf is untainted by water.

(11) Having abandoned attachment, yogins undertake action with the body, mind, and intelligence, even with the senses alone, for the sake of self-purification.

(12) The disciplined man, having abandoned the result of action, attains complete peace; the undisciplined man, whose action is impelled by desire, and who is attached to the result, is bound.

(13) Having renounced all actions with the mind, the embodied self sits easily, ruler in its nine-gated city,* neither acting nor causing action.

(14) The lord of the body does not create agency or actions for the world, or the connection of action and result; rather it is inherent nature that accomplishes this.

(15) The all-pervading lord does not take on the merit or demerit of anyone's actions. Knowledge is concealed by ignorance—and in that way people are deluded.

(16) But for those whose ignorance of the self has been destroyed by knowledge, their knowledge is like the sun, flooding the highest reality with light.

(17) With their intelligences on it, their selves in it, grounded in it, wholly devoted to it, they go never again to be reborn, their impurities shed by knowledge.

(18) Those who know see the same thing in a wise and disciplined brahmin as in a cow or an elephant, or even in a dog or an outcast.

(19) The created world is overcome even here for those whose minds are firmly impartial; for since Brahman is faultless and the same in everything, so they are established in Brahman.

(20) A man should no more rejoice on obtaining what is pleasant than he should become agitated when suffering what is unpleasant. Undeluded, with firm intelligence, the knower of Brahman is established in Brahman.

(21) He whose self is unaffected by outside contact finds his happiness in the self; united through yogic discipline with Brahman, he reaches inextinguishable happiness.

(22) For pleasures deriving from outside contact are sources of unhappiness, Son of Kunti, because they have a

beginning and an end; the wise man takes no delight in them.

(23) The man able to withstand in this world, before liberation from the body, the violent disturbance caused by desire and anger is disciplined and happy.

(24) He who has inner happiness, inner delight, and thereby inner radiance—that yogin, being Brahman, achieves the nirvana of Brahman.*

(25) Seers whose impurities have been destroyed, whose doubts have been dispelled, who have restrained themselves, who delight in the welfare of all beings, reach the nirvana of Brahman.

(26) For those ascetics whose thought is controlled, who have separated themselves from desire and anger, who know themselves, the nirvana of Brahman lies close.

(27) Having excluded outside contacts, fixing his gaze between his eyebrows, making the inward and outward breaths even within the nostrils,

(28) The wise man, whose senses, mind, and intelligence are controlled, who is wholly intent upon release, whose desire, fear, and anger have vanished, is liberated forever.

(29) Realizing that I am the consumer of sacrifices and austerities, the great lord of all the worlds, the companion of all creatures, he attains peace.

CHAPTER 6

The Lord said:

(1) It is the man who undertakes prescribed ritual action, without depending on the results of that action, who is a renouncer and a yogin, not he who has not installed the ritual fire and undertakes no ritual action.

(2) Know, Pandava, that what they call renunciation is in fact yogic discipline; no one at all becomes a yogin unless he has renounced the intention to obtain a particular result.

(3) For the sage who aspires to yogic discipline action is said to be the means; for that man who has already attained yogic discipline quiescence is said to be the means.

(4) For when a man has renounced all intention to obtain a particular result, and clings neither to actions nor to the objects of the senses, he is said to have attained yogic discipline.

(5) A man should raise up the self by the self, he should not drag the self down; for the self is the self's only ally, and the self is the self's only enemy.

(6) For the man whose self has been conquered by the self, the self is the ally of the self; but for the man whose self has not been conquered, the self stands antagonistically, like an opponent.

(7) For the man who has conquered his self and become calm, the supreme self is as firmly concentrated in heat, in cold, in pleasure and pain, as in honour and disgrace.

(8) He whose self is satisfied with knowledge and insight, aloof, his senses subdued, to whom a clod of earth, a stone, and a bar of gold are the same, is called disciplined, a yogin.

(9) The man who has the same mental attitude towards friends, allies, enemies, neutrals, arbiters, the hateful, and kinsmen—towards the good and the evil alike—is set apart.

(10) A yogin should always discipline himself, remaining solitary, his self and thought restrained, desireless and possessionless.

(11) Having established a fixed position for himself in an undefiled place, neither too high nor too low, and covered with a cloth, a skin, or grass,

(12) Sitting there, having made the mind one-pointed, he whose sense activities and thoughts are controlled, should practise yoga to purify the self.

(13) Firm, motionless, holding body, head, and neck in a straight line, focusing on the tip of his own nose, not looking around him,

(14) Tranquil, free from fear, locked in a vow of chastity, controlling his mind, his thought on me, disciplined, he should sit intent on me.

(15) So continually disciplining himself, the yogin whose mind is controlled attains to the tranquillity whose furthest point is nirvana, and rests in me.

(16) Yoga is not for the over-eater, Arjuna, nor for him who does not eat at all; it is not for him in the habit of over-sleeping, nor for him who keeps himself awake.

(17) But for him whose food and recreation are properly disciplined, whose exertions are channelled in activities, who is disciplined in his sleeping and waking, there is the yoga which destroys suffering.

(18) When his controlled thought concentrates on the self alone, free from longing for any desirable objects, then he is called yogically disciplined.

(19) 'Like an unflickering lamp stationed in a draught-proof place'—that is the familiar simile for the yogin whose thought is controlled, practising the discipline of the self.

(20) When thought ceases, checked by the practice of yoga, and a man, seeing the self in the self, is satisfied with himself,

(21) When he knows that infinite bliss which is to be had by the intelligence beyond the senses, established in which he does not waver in the least from the way things really are,

(22) And having gained which, he believes there is nothing superior to it, then grounded in it, he is not touched even by the deepest suffering.

(23) He should know it is that disjunction from union with suffering which is called 'yoga'; that yoga is to be practised with determination and an undaunted mind.

(24) Comprehensively renouncing desires, which are born out of the intention to produce a particular result, totally restraining the collection of the senses by the mind alone,

(25) He should come to rest gently and gradually, with the intelligence held fast; and having fixed the mind in the self, he should not think of anything at all.

(26) Wheresoever the wandering and unsteady mind strays, restraining it, he shall bring it back from that place to control in the self alone.

(27) For supreme bliss comes to the yogin whose mind has grown calm, whose passion is stilled, who has become Brahman, without taint.

(28) So continually disciplining himself, the stainless yogin easily attains to endless bliss, which is the touch of Brahman.

(29) The man whose self is disciplined in yoga, whose perception is the same everywhere, sees himself in all creatures and all creatures in himself.

(30) For the man who sees me in everything and everything in me, I am not lost for him and he is not lost for me.

(31) That yogin grounded in oneness, who honours me as being in all creatures, whatever his mode of life otherwise, exists in me.

(32) That yogin is considered supreme, Arjuna, who by analogy with his own self sees the same thing everywhere, whether pleasurable or painful.

Arjuna said:

(33) Since everything is unstable, I cannot see the permanent foundation of this yoga that you have called 'sameness', Slayer of Madhu.

(34) For the mind is unsteady, Krishna, tormenting, powerful, unyielding; it is as difficult to restrain as the wind, I suppose.

The Lord said:

(35) Without doubt, Great Arm, the mind is hard to control and unsteady, but by repeated practice, Son of Kunti, and by cultivating indifference to passion, it can be held in check.

(36) I agree that it is difficult to achieve yogic discipline if you lack self-restraint, but for the man who strives and is self-controlled there are means by which it can be achieved.

Arjuna said:

(37) Krishna, what path does a man take who is not an ascetic, who possesses faith, yet whose mind has wandered away from discipline without attaining perfection in yoga?

(38) Perhaps, fallen from both, he is destroyed, like a detached cloud, great-armed Krishna—a man without foundation, uncertain on the path of Brahman.

(39) You must completely dispel my doubt, Krishna, for surely only *you* can dispel this doubt.

The Lord said:

(40) Partha, neither in this world nor another is he destroyed; for no one who does good treads an evil path, my friend.

(41) Having attained the worlds that are made by merit, and having dwelt there for countless years, the man who has fallen from yogic discipline is born into a fortunate and pure family.

(42) Or rather he is born into a family of learned yogins, although it is very hard to attain such a birth in this world.

(43) There he resumes that connection with the intelligence which was his in his former body, and then he strives even more for perfection, Son of Kuru.

(44) For even when he is not consciously in control, he is sustained precisely by his previous practice. Even the person who just has a *desire* to know yoga goes beyond the word-Brahman.*

(45) But striving with great effort, the yogin whose defilement has been purified is perfected through many lives, and then he attains the highest goal.

(46) The yogin is superior to mortifiers of the flesh; he is considered superior even to men of knowledge; the yogin is superior to those engaged in action. Therefore, be a yogin, Arjuna!

(47) Moreover, of all yogins it is the one possessing faith, who shares in me, with his inner self given over to me, whom I consider to be the most disciplined.

CHAPTER 7

The Lord said:

(1) Partha, hear how, practising yogic discipline with your mind intent on me, dependent on me, you shall know me entirely and unreservedly.

(2) I shall tell you in full about this knowledge and insight; once you know this, nothing more remains to be known in this world.

(3) Among thousands of men there is hardly one who strives for perfection; even of those who have striven successfully scarcely one knows me in reality.

(4) My material nature is divided into eight: earth, air, fire, wind, ether, mind, intelligence, and ego.

(5) This is my lower nature, but know, Great Arm, my other, higher nature by which this universe is sustained, consisting of sentient beings.*

(6) Understand that this is the source of all living beings; I am the origin and dissolution of this whole universe.

(7) Dhananjaya, there is nothing at all higher than me; all this is strung on me like pearls on a thread.

(8) Son of Kunti, I am taste in the waters, light in the moon and sun, the sacred syllable in all the Vedas, sound in the air, manhood in men.

(9) Also I am the pleasant fragrance in the earth, the radiance in fire, the life in all beings, and in ascetics I am austerity.

(10) Know, Partha, that I am the eternal seed of all creatures, I am the intelligence of the intelligent; I am the brilliance of the brilliant.

(11) And I am the strength of the mighty, freed from passion and desire. In beings I am that desire which does not run counter to proper conduct, Bull of the Bharatas.

(12) And know that all conditions of existence, whether purely, passionately, or darkly constituted, come from me; but I am not in them, they are in me.

(13) The entire universe is deluded by these conditions, derived from the three constituents; it is not aware of me, eternal and beyond them.

(14) For it is hard to go beyond this divine appearance of mine, composed of the constituents; only those who turn to me alone overcome this appearance.

(15) Deluded evil-doers, the worst of men, do not turn to me; their knowledge has been swept away by appearance, dependent as they are upon a demonic mode of existence.

(16) Arjuna, four kinds of good men share in me: the oppressed, the man who desires knowledge, the man whose object is prosperity, and the one who knows, Bull of the Bharatas.

(17) Of these, the continuously disciplined knower, whose devotion is exclusive, is outstanding, for I am extraordinarily dear to the man who knows, and he is dear to me.

(18) Indeed, these four are all illustrious, but the knower I consider to be myself, for the man who disciplines himself exists in me, the incomparable situation.

(19) It is only after many births that the possessor of knowledge turns to me, realizing that Vasudeva* is everything. So great a spirit is very hard to find.

(20) Those whose knowledge has been charmed away by this or that desire turn to other gods, following this or that injunction, ruled by their own natures.

(21) Yet, whatever the divine form, any devotee who aspires to worship it with faith is unshakeably established in that faith by me.

(22) The man who is bound up in that faith longs to propitiate such a god and thereby attain his desires—desires fulfilled by me alone.

(23) Yet for those whose understanding is limited, the reward is limited. Those who worship the gods go to the gods, but those who are devoted to me go to me.

(24) The unintelligent think of me, the unmanifest, as reduced to manifestation, oblivious of my higher state, which is unchanging and incomparable.

(25) Clothed in the appearance created by my yogic power, I am not clearly visible to all; this deluded world does not recognize me as unchanging and unborn.

(26) Arjuna, I know the dead, the living, and those creatures yet to come, but no one at all knows me.

(27) Confused by duality, which arises from desire and hatred, all creatures in existence fall into delusion, Bharata, Incinerator of the Foe.

(28) But there are men whose actions are pure, for whom evil has come to an end; liberated from the confusion of duality, they devote themselves to me, and their vows are solid.

(29) Those who strive for liberation from old age and death, relying upon me, know this Brahman in its entirety, in relation to the self, and the totality of action.

(30) And those who know me in relation to beings and in relation to the divine, as well as in relation to the sacrifice, have disciplined minds, and know me even in the hour of death.

CHAPTER 8

Arjuna said:

(1) What is that 'Brahman'? What is 'in relation to the self'? What is 'action', Supreme Person? And what are labelled 'in relation to beings' and 'in relation to the divine'?

(2) Here, in this body, who is 'in relation to the sacrifice'? And in what way, Destroyer of Madhu? And how, in the hour of death, can you be known by the self-controlled?

The Lord said:

(3) Supreme Brahman is the imperishable; in relation to the self it is said to be inherent nature. The creative power which brings about the existence of creatures is called action.

(4) In relation to beings it is the transitory state, in relation to the divine, the spirit; in relation to sacrifice it is I myself here in the body, best of embodied beings.

(5) And whoever dies, remembering me alone at the moment of death, attains to my state once he is liberated from the body—there can be no doubt about that.

(6) Indeed, whatever state he calls to mind as he abandons his body at its end, he inevitably attains it, Son of Kunti, transmuted to that state.

(7) Therefore think of me at all times and fight. With your intelligence and mind fixed in me, you will certainly come to me.

(8) With his thought disciplined by the practice of yoga, concentrating on the divine supreme person and not straying towards anything else, a man goes to him, Partha.

(9–10) Whoever, disciplined with the power of yoga and with devotion, having correctly installed his vital breath between his eyebrows, meditates, with an unwavering mind at the time of death, on the primordial seer, the ruler who is subtler than the subtle, the supporter of everything, unimaginable in form, the colour of the sun beyond darkness, goes to that divine supreme person.

(11) Now I shall tell you briefly about that state which those who know the Veda call the imperishable, which strivers who are free from passion enter, and desiring which they lead a celibate life.

(12) Having shut all the body's doors and confined his mind in his heart, having installed his vital breath in his head, a man is fixed in yogic concentration.

(13) The man who, abandoning the body, dies pronouncing the one-syllabled Brahman, '*Om*',* while thinking on me, attains the highest goal.

(14) For the perpetually disciplined yogin who continuously thinks on me, and whose mind is never anywhere else, I am easy to reach, Partha.

(15) Having reached me, great souls do not suffer that impermanent receptacle of suffering, rebirth; they have attained the highest perfection.

(16) Up to Brahma's realm,* Arjuna, the worlds come round again and again; but once I have been reached, Son of Kunti, rebirth is finished.

(17) Those men know day and night who know that a day of Brahma lasts for a thousand ages, just as a Brahma night ends after a thousand ages.

(18) As day dawns everything manifest emerges from the unmanifest; as night falls it merges back into that same designated unmanifest.*

(19) This troop of beings, having come into being again and again, ineluctably merges back at nightfall; and at dawn it emerges again, Partha.

(20) But there is another state of being beyond this unmanifest, an eternal unmanifest which, when all creatures are destroyed, is not itself destroyed.

(21) The unmanifest called 'imperishable'—that, they say, is the highest goal. Once attained, there is no coming back from it—that is my supreme domain.

(22) It is the supreme person, Partha, to be attained by exclusive devotion; beings exist within it; this whole universe is displayed on it.

(23) I shall tell you, Bull of the Bharatas, those times at which yogins, passing from this life, return, or go not to return.

(24) Men who know Brahman, departing by fire, by light, by day, in the bright lunar fortnight, and during the six months of the sun's northern path go to Brahman.

(25) The yogin who has attained the moon's light by smoke, by night, in the dark lunar fortnight, and during the six months of the sun's southern path returns.*

(26) For the universe these light and dark paths are considered eternal: via one a man goes not to return, via the other he returns again.

(27) Arjuna, the yogin who knows these two paths is not in the least confused; you should, therefore, at all times be yogically disciplined.

(28) With regard to the Vedas, to sacrifices, to ascetic practices, and to gifts the recompense of merit is fixed: the yogin who knows goes beyond all that and attains to the supreme, original state.

CHAPTER 9

The Lord said:

(1) But I shall relate to you, who are free of ill will, the most secret knowledge and insight; knowing it you shall be freed from harm.

(2) It is royal knowledge, a royal secret, the greatest purification, directly experienced, conforming to what is right, easy to practise, permanent.

(3) Men who have no faith in this truth, Incinerator of the Foe, fail to reach me and are returned to the rut of recurrent death.

(4) This entire universe is displayed on me in my unmanifest form; all creatures exist in me, but I do not exist in them.

(5) And yet creatures do *not* exist in me—behold my superhuman yogic power! My self causes creatures to exist, and maintains them, but it does not exist in them.

(6) In the way that the great wind blows everywhere and yet remains perpetually within space, so, you must suppose, all creatures exist within me.

(7) Son of Kunti, all creatures re-enter my material nature at the end of a world cycle,* and at the beginning of a cycle I emit them again.

(8) Supported by my own material nature, time after time I emit this entire, powerless multitude of creatures through the power of nature.

(9) And these actions do not bind me, Dhananjaya; seated like a neutral, I am unattached to such actions.

(10) With me as a supervisor, material nature generates moving and unmoving creatures; that is the reason the universe goes round, Son of Kunti.

(11) When I take on a human form the deluded do not recognize me, ignorant of my higher state as the great lord of creatures.

(12) Dependent upon a deluding, demoniacal, and evil nature, their hopes, actions, and knowledge are futile and mindless.

(13) But the great-souled, Partha, grounded in divine material nature, worship me single-mindedly, realizing that I am the imperishable origin of creatures.

(14) There are those whose vows are solid who, continually glorifying me, striving, and bowing to me with devotion, ever-disciplined, worship me.

(15) And there are others, sacrificing with the sacrifice of knowledge, who worship me as the one, the separate, the various, facing in every direction.

(16) I am the ritual, I am the sacrifice, I am the offering to the ancestors, I am the herb, I am the mantra, I am the clarified butter, I am the fire, I am the oblation.

(17) I am the father of this world, the mother, the maintainer, the grandfather, the object of knowledge, the purifying filter, the syllable *Om*, the Rig, the Sama, and the Yajur Vedas too.*

(18) Path, bearer, lord, witness, home, refuge, friend, origin, dissolution, continuity, repository, imperishable seed,

(19) I radiate, I withhold the rain, and I let it come down, I am immortality, and death, I am the existent, and the non-existent, Arjuna.

(20) The knowers of the three Vedas, soma-drinkers,* whose sins have been cleansed, having offered to me with sacrifices, strive to attain the goal of heaven; and having reached the pure world of Indra,* they partake in heaven of the divine pleasures of the gods.

(21) Thus having enjoyed that vast world of heaven, when their merit is used up they re-enter the mortal world, and so conforming to the three Vedas, desiring desires, they come and go.

(22) But to those men who honour me, concentrating on me alone, who are constantly disciplined, I bring gain and security.

(23) Even those who are devotees of other gods, and sacrifice to them full of faith, really sacrifice to me, Son of Kunti, albeit not according to the prescribed rules.

(24) For I am the lord, and the recipient of all sacrifices, although they do not truly recognize me, and so they slide.

(25) Those who have vowed themselves to the gods go to the gods, those whose vows are to the fathers go to the fathers, those worshipping spirits go to spirits, and those who sacrifice to me go to me.

(26) I accept a leaf, a flower, a fruit, or water from the disciplined person who, with devotion, offers me that loving offering.

(27) Whatever you do, whatever you eat, whatever you offer, whatever you give away, whatever asceticism you perform, Son of Kunti, do it as an offering to me.

(28) Thus you shall be liberated from good and evil results, from the bonds of action. With your self disciplined by the yoga of renunciation, liberated, you shall come to me.

(29) I am the same with regard to all creatures; I feel neither aversion nor affection. But whoever shares in me with devotion, they are in me and I am in them.

(30) Even the evil-doer, if he shares in me with single-minded devotion, may be thought of as good, for he has fixed on what is right.

(31) He quickly conforms to the true law and attains everlasting peace. You should realize, Son of Kunti, that no devotee of mine is lost.

(32) For whoever depends on me, Partha, however low their origins—whether they are women, farmers and merchants, or even labourers and serfs—they go by the highest path.

(33) How much more then deserving brahmins and devoted royal seers. Since you have been born into this impermanent, unhappy world, devote yourself to me.

(34) Fix your mind on me; and so devoted to me, sacrificing to me, reverencing me, having disciplined your self, with me as your final resort, you shall come to me.

CHAPTER 10

The Lord said:

(1) Once more, Great Arm, listen to my supreme word, which I shall utter to gladden you, out of a desire to do you good.

(2) Neither the congregation of gods nor the great seers know my origin, for I am comprehensively the source of the gods and the great seers.

(3) Among mortals, he who knows me as the birthless, beginningless, great lord of the world, is undeluded and liberated from all evils.

(4) Intelligence, knowledge, freedom from delusion, patience, truthfulness, self-control, equanimity, happiness, misery, becoming and non-becoming, fear and fearlessness,

(5) Non-violence, impartiality, contentment, austerity, liberality, honour, and dishonour are various creaturely states that originate from me alone.

(6) The ancient seven great seers, and the four Manus* from whom these beings in the world came, originated from me, born of mind.

(7) Whoever truly knows this manifest all-pervading power and yoga of mine is disciplined by an unshakeable yoga—there can be no doubt about that.

(8) The intelligent, filled with my state of being, share in me, knowing that I am the origin of all this, and that everything unrolls from me.

(9) Their thoughts on me, their life breath directed towards me, enlightening each other and constantly talking of me, they are gratified and rejoice.

(10) To those who are continuously disciplined, who worship me full of joy, I grant the discipline of intelligence by which they come to me.

(11) Situated in their being, out of compassion for them I put to flight the darkness born of their ignorance with the bright lamp of knowledge.

Arjuna said:

(12–13) Lord, the divine seer Narada, and all the seers, along with Asita, Devala, and Vyasa,* call you highest Brahman, highest home, supreme purifier, eternal divine person, the original god, unborn and all-pervading—and you have told me so yourself.

(14) All this you have told me I believe to be the essential truth, Keshava; for neither gods nor demons, Lord, know your manifestation.

(15) You know yourself through yourself alone, Supreme Person, creator of creatures, lord of beings, God of gods, lord of the universe.

(16) Give me a complete catalogue of your divine, manifest, all-pervading power—manifestations through which, having pervaded the worlds, you continue in them.

(17) Yogin, how, in constant meditation, may I know you? And in what various states of being should I meditate on you, Lord?

(18) Tell me again, in detail, of your power and manifestation, Janardana, for I can never hear enough of this immortal discourse.

The Lord said:

(19) Very well, I shall tell you about my divine manifestations—the major ones, Best of Kurus, for I am unbounded.

(20) I am the self, Gudakesha, situated in the hearts of all creatures, just as I am the beginning, the middle, and the end of creatures.*

(21) Of the Adityas* I am Vishnu, of lights the radiant sun, of the Maruts* I am their leader Marichi, of heavenly bodies I am the moon.

(22) Of the Vedas I am the Sama Veda, of the gods I am Indra, of the senses I am the mind,* I am the consciousness of creatures.

(23) Of the Rudras* I am Shiva,* of Yakshas and Rakshasas the Lord of Wealth,* of Vasus* I am Fire, of mountains I am Meru.*

(24) Know, Partha, that of appointed priests I am the chief—Brihaspati,* of army commanders I am Skanda,* of waters I am the ocean.

(25) Of the great seers I am Bhrigu, of speech I am the single syllable *Om*, of sacrifices I am the muttered offering, of immovable things I am the Himalaya.

(26) Among all trees I am the sacred fig tree,* of the divine seers Narada, of the Gandharvas* Chitraratha, of perfected beings the sage Kapila.

(27) Know that of horses I am Ucchaihshravas, born from nectar,* of lordly elephants Airavata, and of men the king.

(28) Of weapons I am the thunderbolt, of cows the Cow of Plenty, procreating I am Kandarpa, the god of love, of snakes I am Vasuki, the serpent king.

(29) Of Naga serpents I am Ananta,* of water creatures I am Varuna,* and of the ancestors I am Aryaman; among those who control I am Yama.*

(30) Of Daityas* I am Prahlada,* of reckoners I am time, of wild animals I am the lion, and of birds Garuda.*

(31) Of purifiers I am the wind, of warriors I am Rama,* and of water monsters I am the crocodile, of rivers I am the Ganges.

(32) Arjuna, I am the beginning, the middle, and the end of creations, the knowledge of supreme self among sciences; I am the discourse of those who speak.

(33) Of letters I am the letter *a*, and of grammatical compounds I am the conjunctive one;* I am indeed undecaying Time, the arranger facing in every direction.

(34) I am death that bears everything away, and the source of what is yet to be. Of feminine things I am fame, prosperity, and speech, memory, intelligence, constancy, and patience.*

(35) In the same way, of Saman chants* I am the Great Saman, of metres the Gayatri,* of months I am the first month, of seasons I am Spring.

(36) I am the dicing of the gamblers, I am the lustre of the lustrous, I am victory, I am purpose, I am the courage of the courageous.

(37) Of the Vrishnis* I am Vasudeva,* of the Pandavas Arjuna, of the sages I am Vyasa,* of poets I am Ushanas.*

(38) I am the stick of the chastisers, I am the strategy of those who seek to win, I am the silence of secret things, and the knowledge of those who know.

(39) I am that which is the seed of all beings, Arjuna. There could be no creatures, moving or unmoving, without me.

(40) There is no end to my divine manifestations, Incinerator of the Foe. I have spoken merely to let you sample the extent of my manifest power.

(41) You should know that whatever being manifests abundant power, prosperity, or strength, in every instance it derives from a spark of my lustre.

(42) But of what use is this wide-ranging knowledge to you, Arjuna? Supporting this entire universe with a single fragment of myself, I subsist.

CHAPTER 11

Arjuna said:

(1) What you have said, as a favour to me, about the supreme mystery in relation to the self, has dispelled my delusion.

(2) From you, lotus-eyed one, I have heard in full detail about the generation and dissolution of beings, and your indissoluble greatness.

(3) In this way, lord in the highest degree, you have described your self; I desire to see your supreme form, greatest of persons.

(4) Lord, if you think I am capable of seeing it, then, great lord of yoga, show me your indissoluble self.

The Lord said:

(5) Partha, see my hundredfold and thousandfold forms—diverse, divine, variegated, and manifold.

(6) See the Adityas, Vasus, Rudras, the twin Ashvins, and the Maruts.* See, Bharata, many prodigious things, never witnessed before.

(7) Now see, Gudakesha, here in my body the entire universe of moving and unmoving things, and whatever else you desire to behold.

(8) But you will not be able to see me with your natural eye, so I give you a divine eye—behold my lordly power!

Sanjaya said:

(9) Then, O king, Hari, the great lord of yoga, revealed to Partha his lordly, supreme form.

(10) It had many mouths and eyes, innumerable wonderful aspects, uncounted divine ornaments, countless divine weapons at the ready;

(11) It was wearing divine garlands and robes, divine perfumes and ointments; it was made up of every prodigious thing; divine, infinite, facing in every direction.

(12) If the light of a thousand suns should all at once rise into the sky, that might approach the brilliance of that great self.

(13) The son of Pandu saw the entire universe, in its multiplicity, gathered there as one in the body of the god of gods.

(14) Then Dhananjaya, confounded, his hair bristling, bowed his head to the god, and with his hands joined in reverence said:

Arjuna said:

(15) O God, I see in your body the gods and all kinds of beings come together, Lord Brahma* on his lotus seat, all the seers and the divine serpents.

(16) I see you everywhere, many-armed, many-stomached, many-mouthed, many-eyed, infinite in form; I cannot find out your end, your middle or your beginning—Lord of the universe, form of everything.

(17) I see you—so hard to behold—crowned, armed with a club, discus-bearing, a mass of radiant energy, blazing in all directions, unlimited, an all-consuming, fiery, solar brilliance.

(18) I acknowledge you as the imperishable, the highest object of knowledge: you are the repository of all this, the unchanging protector of the perpetual law. You are the primeval person.

(19) Without beginning, middle, or end, infinite in power, infinite in arms, sun and moon-eyed, I see you, your face a blazing fire, consuming the entire universe with your brilliance.

(20) This space between heaven and earth is filled by you alone, as is every direction. Having seen this, your marvellous, terrible form, the three worlds* totter—Great Self!

(21) Those throngs of gods enter you; some, in dread, praise you with gestures of respect. Crying, 'Hail!' crowds of great seers and perfected beings praise you with resounding praise.

(22) Rudras and Adityas, Vasus and Sadhyas, the Vishva gods, the twin Ashvins, Maruts, steam-drinkers, crowds of celestial musicians, Yakshas, Asuras and perfected beings all gaze at you, dumbfounded.*

(23) Great Arm, seeing your mighty form with its many mouths and eyes, its many arms, thighs, and feet, its many stomachs, its gaping mouths, full of tusks—the worlds reel, and so do I.

(24) Vishnu, seeing you touching the sky, shining, rainbow-hued, cavern-mouthed, with luminous distended eyes, I am shaken to the core; I can find neither resolution nor rest.

(25) Seeing your mouths dancing with tusks, like the flames of universal dissolution, I am disorientated and without shelter. Have mercy, lord of gods, home of the world!

(26) And all those sons of Dhritarashtra,* with crowds of kings—Bhishma, Drona, and the charioteer's son*—together with our foremost warriors too,

(27) Flow into your terrifying fang-distended mouths. Some can be seen lodged between your teeth, their heads crushed to a pulp.

(28) As many river currents converge on the sea, so those heroes of the human world flow into your blazing mouths.

(29) As flying insects propel themselves to death in the brilliant flame, so the worlds impetuously hurl themselves to destruction between your jaws.

(30) Vishnu, you lap up all the worlds with your flaming mouths, ubiquitously devouring; your fierce rays engulf the entire universe in brilliance, roasting it.

(31) Tell me, terrible manifestation, who are you? Homage to you, supreme god—have mercy! First being, I need to understand you; I cannot discern your purpose.

The Lord said:

(32) I am time run on, destroyer of the universe, risen here to annihilate worlds. Regardless of you, all these warriors, stationed in opposing ranks, shall cease to exist.

(33) Therefore go to it, grasp fame! And having conquered your enemies, enjoy a thriving kingship. They have already been hewn down by me: Savyasachin, simply be the instrument.

(34) Kill Drona, kill Bhishma, kill Jayadratha and Karna,* and the other warrior heroes as well: they are killed by me. Don't waver—you must fight! In battle you shall overcome your enemies.

Sanjaya said:

(35) When he had heard Krishna's speech, Arjuna, his palms joined in reverence, trembling, having saluted again, bowing low, terrified, stuttered in reply:

Arjuna said:

(36) It is only right, Hrishikesha, that the world exults in and is devoted to your celebration. Terrified demons scatter to the

winds, and all the crowds of perfected beings bow down before you.

(37) And how should they not bow down to you, Great One? To the original creator, greater even than Brahma,* infinite lord of gods, home of the world. You are the imperishable—being, non-being, and what is beyond.

(38) You are the original god, the primeval person; you are the receptacle of all this—knower, known, and ultimate condition. Infinite form, the entire universe was composed by you.

(39) You are Vayu, Yama, Agni, Varuna, the moon, Prajapati, the great grandfather.* Praise, a thousand times praise to you; again and again, praise and praise you.

(40) Praise to you openly, secretly, totally—the All! Infinite strength, unmeasured force, completing everything, you are everything.

(41) For whatever I uttered rashly, imagining you my equal, calling: 'Hey Krishna! Hey Yadava! Hey friend!' ignorant of your greatness, through familiarity, or out of affection—

(42) And if as a joke I treated you improperly when it came to sport, rest, sitting, or eating, alone or even in public, Achyuta—I ask you, the Immeasurable, forgiveness.

(43) You are the father of the world, of moving and unmoving things; you are its venerable teacher and object of worship. Nothing can be compared to you, so how, even in the three worlds, could there be anything greater? Unequalled power!

(44) Therefore, bowing down and prostrating myself, I ask forgiveness of you, praiseworthy lord. As father with son, friend with friend, lover with lover, have patience—if it pleases you—O god!

(45) I rejoice that I have seen what has never before been seen, but my mind is unhinged with fear. O god, show me that other form again. Be merciful, lord of gods, home of the world!

(46) I need to see you as you were before: crowned, with a club, and holding a discus. O thousand-armed one, whose material form is the universe, assume your four-armed shape.*

The Lord said:

(47) By showing favour to you, Arjuna, through my own power I have made manifest this supreme form of mine, lustrous,

universal, infinite, primeval, which no one apart from you has ever seen.

(48) Not through the Vedas, not through sacrifice, not through study, not by giving alms, not by rituals, not by fierce asceticism, can I be seen in such a form in the human world; by you alone it can be seen, Prince of Kurus.

(49) Don't tremble, don't be confused because you have seen this so terrible form of mine. Your dread dispelled, your heart lightened, behold this, my familiar form.

Sanjaya said:

(50) So saying, Vasudeva once more revealed his own familiar form to Arjuna; the Great One, resuming his mild appearance, allowed the terrified man to breathe again.

Arjuna said:

(51) Seeing this agreeable, human form of yours, Janardana, I have now pulled myself together, and I am rational again.

The Lord said:

(52) This form of mine, which you have seen, is very hard to see. Even the gods crave incessantly for a glimpse of this form.

(53) Neither through the Vedas, nor through asceticism, neither by alms-giving, nor by sacrifice is it possible to see me in the way you have seen me.

(54) But by exclusive devotion, Arjuna, I can be known and seen thus, as I really am, and entered into, Incinerator of the Foe.

(55) He who acts for me, who makes me the highest goal, who is devoted to me, who has abandoned attachment, who is without hatred for any being, comes to me, Pandava.

CHAPTER 12

Arjuna said:

(1) So between those who are ever-disciplined, who are devoted to you and attend on you, and those who pursue the imperishable unmanifest, who are the most expert in yoga?

The Lord said:

(2) I consider the most expert in yoga to be those who, ever-disciplined, having fixed their minds on me, attend on me filled with the highest faith.

(3) Yet those who attend on the indefinable, imperishable unmanifest, ubiquitous and inconceivable, unchanging, unmoving, embedded,

(4) Who, controlling all their senses, are equably minded in all circumstances, and take pleasure in the welfare of all creatures, they too attain to me.

(5) The barrier for those whose thoughts are attached to the unmanifest is greater, for it is not easy for the embodied to attain an unmanifest goal.

(6) But for those who resign every action to me, who, intent on me and meditating on me, with exclusive discipline worship me,

(7) I am the one who rapidly hauls them out of the ocean of death and continual rebirth, Partha, for their thoughts are engrossed in me.

(8) Fix your mind on me alone, let your intelligence enter me: you *will* live in me thereafter, there is no doubt of that.

(9) Or if you cannot manage to fix your thought unwaveringly on me, then you must try to attain me through persistent yogic practice, Dhananjaya.

(10) Yet even if you are incapable of persistent practice, you should concentrate on acting for me; simply by acting for my sake you will attain success.

(11) And if even this is beyond your powers, then, taking refuge in my yogic discipline, restrain yourself and abandon the fruit of all your actions.

(12) For knowledge is better than study, meditation is superior to knowledge, the abandonment of the fruit of actions is better than meditation, and after abandonment peace immediately follows.

(13) Without hatred for any creature, friendly and compassionate, free from possessiveness and egoism, indifferent to pleasure and pain, enduring,

(14) Contented, ever the self-controlled yogin, certain of purpose, his mind and intelligence concentrated on me, he who is devoted to me is dear to me.

(15) He is dear to me who does not afflict the world and is not afflicted by it—who is free from excitement, impatience, fear, and anxiety.

(16) He is dear to me who, devoted to me, is disinterested, pure, able, non-partisan, unworried, and does not initiate any actions.

(17) He is dear to me who, filled with devotion, is neither excited nor repelled by things, neither grieves nor gives way to longing, and who abandons both the auspicious and the inauspicious.

(18–19) The man is dear to me who, filled with devotion, is the same with regard to enemies and friends, in honour and dishonour, the same in heat and cold, pleasure and suffering, who, freed from attachment, weighs blame and praise the same, who is silent, satisfied in all circumstances, homeless, and firm-minded.

(20) And above all, those devotees are dear to me who, full of faith, with me as their highest object, attend to this immortal nectar of truth, which I have just delivered to you.

CHAPTER 13

The Lord said:

(1) Son of Kunti, this body is called 'the field', and the one who knows it is 'the knower of the field'—so those who are expert in this say.

(2) You should know, Bharata, that in all fields I am the knower of the field. Knowledge of the knower and of the field—that is what I consider knowledge.

(3) What this field is, what its characteristics and mutations are, and how they come about, who the knower is, and what his powers are, hear from me in short.

(4) It has been chanted distinctly by the seers in many ways, and in various metres, and it has been given expression in aphorisms about Brahman with compelling reasons.

(5) The gross elements, the ego, the intelligence, and the unmanifest, the eleven faculties, and the five realms of the senses,*

(6) Desire, aversion, pleasure, pain, the bodily organism, consciousness, and will—these in short are designated the field and its modifications.

(7) Lack of pride, lack of deceit, non-violence, endurance, sincerity, serving one's teacher, purity, stability, self-control,

(8) Dispassion with regard to the objects of the senses, freedom from egoism, perceiving the deficiencies of birth, death, old age, disease, and pain,

(9) Non-attachment, distancing oneself from sons, wife, the home, etc., and constant even-mindedness in the face of pleasing or unpleasing events,

(10) Unswerving devotion to me through exclusive yogic discipline, seeking out an isolated place, dissatisfaction with the society of men,

(11) Constancy in knowledge of what relates to the self, perceiving the purpose of knowledge of reality—this, it is declared, constitutes knowledge; anything opposed to this is ignorance.

(12) I shall tell you of that object of knowledge, knowing which one reaches immortality—beginningless, supreme Brahman, characterized as neither existent nor non-existent.

(13) Hands and feet everywhere, eyes, head, and face everywhere, ears everywhere, covering everything in the world it stands.

(14) Appearing to have all sense qualities, it is free of all senses, detached and yet supporting everything, devoid of the constituents and yet experiencing them.

(15) Outside and inside creatures, unmoving and moving, too subtle for comprehension, it is both present and remote.

(16) Existing in creatures as though divided, yet undivided, it should be known as the sustainer, swallower, and source of creatures.

(17) It is called the light of lights beyond darkness—knowledge, the object of knowledge, and the goal of knowledge, inherent in the heart of everyone.

(18) Thus the field, knowledge, and the object of knowledge have been succinctly described: realizing this, my devotee arrives at my state.

(19) You must know that material nature and the person are both beginningless, and know that the modifications and the constituents also arise from material nature.

(20) Material nature, it is said, is the reason for cause and effect and agency; the person is said to be the cause in the experiencing of happiness and unhappiness.

(21) For the person situated in material nature experiences the constituents arising from material nature: its attachment to the constituents causes it to be born in good and bad wombs.

(22) The highest person in this body is called witness, consenter, supporter, experiencer, the Great Lord, the Supreme Self.

(23) He who thus knows the person, and material nature together with its constituents, is not born again whatever his present condition.

(24) There are some who by meditation see the self in the self themselves, others do so by the discipline of Sankhya,* and others again by the discipline of action.

(25) And there are some, not knowing these ways, who nevertheless esteem what they have heard from others, and, revering what they hear, they too go beyond death.

(26) You should know, Bull of the Bharatas, that any being whatever, whether moving or stationary, is born from the union of the field and the knower of the field.

(27) He who sees the Supreme Lord as situated equally in all creatures, not perishing when they perish, he *sees.*

(28) For seeing the Lord equally present everywhere, he cannot through himself injure the self, and so he takes the highest path.

(29) And he who sees that actions are performed exclusively by material nature, and that the self is therefore not the agent, *sees*.

(30) When he perceives the various separate states of being as existing in the one, and extending from that alone, he attains Brahman.

(31) This Supreme, imperishable Self, because it has no beginning and no constituents, even though it exists in the body, Son of Kunti, does not act and is not polluted.

(32) Just as the all-pervading ether is not polluted because of its subtlety, so the self, although it is present in every body, is not polluted.

(33) Just as the one sun lights up this entire world, so, Bharata, the owner of the field lights the entire field.

(34) Those who with the eye of knowledge thus know the difference between the field and the knower of the field, and the way in which creatures are liberated from material nature, attain to the highest.

CHAPTER 14

The Lord said:

(1) Again I shall teach you the supreme knowledge—the best of knowledges—knowing which, all sages have gone from here to the supreme attainment.

(2) Relying upon this knowledge, they have reached my level of existence, and even at the beginning of a cycle of creation they are not reborn, nor do they cease to be at its dissolution.

(3) Great Brahman is my womb, in it I place the embryo; the origin of all creatures derives from that, Bharata.

(4) Whatever forms are produced in any wombs, Son of Kunti, Brahman is their great womb and I am the seed-giving father.

(5) Purity, passion, and darkness, the constituents arising out of material nature, bind the imperishable embodied self to the body, Great Arm.

(6) Of these, purity, being free from taint, is illuminating and healthy; it binds through attachment to the pleasant and through attachment to knowledge, sinless Arjuna.

(7) Son of Kunti, know that passion is characterized by desire, arising out of craving and attachment; it binds the embodied self through an attachment to action.

(8) But know that darkness is born from ignorance, perplexing all embodied selves; it binds through negligence, indolence, and sleep, Bharata.

(9) Purity causes attachment to the pleasant, passion to action, Bharata; but darkness, by obscuring knowledge, causes attachment to negligence.

(10) Having overcome passion and darkness, purity prevails, Bharata; as does passion, having overcome purity and darkness, and darkness, having overcome purity and passion.

(11) When the light that is knowledge is produced in all the apertures in this body, then one knows that purity has prevailed.

(12) Greed, exertion, the undertaking of actions, restlessness, ambition: these appear when passion prevails, Bull of the Bharatas.

(13) Obscurity and indolence, negligence and delusion appear when darkness prevails, Joy of the Kurus.

(14) When the embodied self dies during the dominance of purity, then it enters the unpolluted worlds of those who know the highest.

(15) Having died in passion, it is born among those attached to action; similarly, dying in darkness it is born among the wombs of the doltish.

(16) They say that the result of properly performed action has the nature of purity and is unpolluted; but the result of passion is suffering, and the fruit of darkness, ignorance.

(17) From purity comes knowledge, and from passion greed, from darkness come negligence and delusion, as well as ignorance.

(18) Those established in purity go upwards, the passionate stand in the middle, those fixed in darkness, the lowest mode of the constituents, go below.

(19) When one who sees clearly recognizes that there is no agent other than the constituents, and realizes what is higher than the constituents, he attains to my state of being.

(20) Having gone beyond these three constituents, which are the sources of the body, the embodied self, released from birth, death, old age, and suffering, attains immortality.

Arjuna said:

(21) By what distinguishing characteristics is the man who has transcended these three constituents recognized, Mighty Lord? How does he conduct himself? And how does he go beyond these three constituents?

The Lord said:

(22) Pandava, he is neither averse to illumination, activity, nor delusion when they have arisen, nor desires them when they have ceased.

(23–25) The man sitting apart, disinterested, unmoved by the constituents, saying to himself, 'It is the constituents that are operating,' who stands firm and does not waver, to whom pain and pleasure are the same, who is self-possessed, to whom a clod of earth, a stone, and a piece of gold come alike, to whom the pleasant and the unpleasant and blame and praise are equal, who is constant, who is indifferent to honour and dishonour, impartial towards friendly or hostile factions, and who has renounced all undertakings, is said to have gone beyond the constituents.

(26) And the man who with unswerving discipline of devotion serves me, having gone beyond these constituents, is fit to become Brahman.

(27) For I am the foundation of Brahman, of the immortal and imperishable, of the eternal law, and of absolute bliss.

CHAPTER 15

The Lord said:

(1) They speak of the eternal Ashvattha,* roots above, branches below, whose leaves are the Vedic hymns; who knows it knows the Veda.

(2) Its branches extend below and above, nurtured by the constituents; its shoots are the objects of the senses, and its roots, extending below, connect with action in the human world.

(3–4) Here its form cannot be perceived, neither its end, nor its beginning, nor its continuity. Having cut this so maturely rooted Ashvattha tree with the strong axe of non-attachment, you should then seek out that place from which, once they have attained it, men never again return—'I take refuge with that primal person from whom original activity issued out.'

(5) The unperplexed, who are free from pride and delusion, whose failings of attachment have been overcome, who are continually concerned with what relates to the self, whose desires have been extinguished, freed from dualities—from pleasure and pain—go to that imperishable place.

(6) The sun does not light it, nor the moon, nor fire. Those who have attained it do not return. It is my highest home.

(7) In the world of living souls, a small part of me, becoming an individual eternal soul, draws to itself the five senses and the mind, which exist in material nature.

(8) When the lord takes on a body and when he steps up out of it, taking these with him, he goes like the wind, bearing perfumes from their source.

(9) Overseeing hearing, sight, touch, taste, smell, and the mind, he makes use of the objects of the senses.

(10) Whether he goes or stays, or experiences via his connection with the constituents, the perplexed do not perceive him; but those with the eye of knowledge do.

(11) Yogins, striving, see him established in themselves, but, even if they strive, the mindless, who are incomplete in themselves, do not see him.

(12) That radiance contained in the sun, which lights up the entire universe, which is in the moon and in fire—know that that radiance is mine.

(13) And having penetrated the earth, I support creatures with my vitality; and having become Soma,* the essence of flavour, I nourish every herb.

(14) Having become the fire of digestion, dwelling in the body of breathing creatures, joined with the in and out breaths, I consume the four kinds of food.

(15) I am fixed in the hearts of all; from me come memory, knowledge, and reasoning; I am to be known through all the Vedas, I make the Vedanta,* I know the Veda.

(16) In the world there are two persons—the perishable and the imperishable. All creatures are perishable, the aloof they call the imperishable.

(17) But there is another, higher person, called the Supreme Self, the eternal lord who, penetrating the three worlds, sustains them.

(18) As I go beyond the perishable and am even higher than the imperishable, so I am celebrated in the world and the Veda as the Supreme Person.

(19) So he who, unperplexed, knows me as the Supreme Person, is all-knowing and shares in me with his entire being, Bharata.

(20) Thus I have articulated this most mysterious doctrine, Blameless One; being awakened to this a man may become wise and will have fulfilled his purpose, Bharata.

CHAPTER 16

The Lord said:

(1) Fearlessness, purity of character, perseverence in the discipline of knowledge, giving, self-control, and sacrifice, recitation of the Veda, asceticism, uprightness,

(2) Non-violence, truthfulness, freedom from anger, renunciation, tranquillity, absence of calumny, compassion for creatures, freedom from greed, gentleness, modesty, steadiness,

(3) Vigour, patience, resolution, purity, freedom from malice and excessive pride—these, Bharata, belong to the man born to a divine fulfilment.

(4) Hypocrisy, pride, haughtiness, anger, harshness, and ignorance belong to the man born to a demonic fulfilment, Partha.

(5) It is believed that the divine fulfilment leads to release, the demonic to bondage. Do not worry, Pandava, you were born to a divine fulfilment.

(6) There are two kinds of creation in this world—the divine and the demonic. I have spoken at length on the divine, now hear me on the demonic, Partha.

(7) Demonic men do not understand activity and renunciation of activity; neither purity, nor good conduct, nor truth is to be found in them.

(8) They claim that the world is devoid of reality, without a foundation, godless, that it is not the product of successive causation. How else is it caused, you may ask? Simply by desire, they say.

(9) Holding rigidly to this view, they rise up for the destruction of the world, despoilers who have lost themselves, whose actions are savage and whose intelligence is limited.

(10) Subject to insatiable desire, filled with intoxicating hypocrisy and pride, having fastened onto false views through delusion, they follow polluting rules of conduct.

(11) Obsessed with an unbounded care, which only ends in death, the summit of their ambition is to gratify their desires, convinced that that is everything.

(12) Bound by a hundred cords of expectation, possessed by desire and anger, unjustly they seek stacks of wealth to gratify their desires.

(13) 'I have attained this today, and I *shall* attain this wish too. So much is mine now, and still more shall be mine in the future.

(14) 'That opponent has already been killed by me, and I shall kill others. I am a lord, I am a consumer, I am a success, I am powerful and happy.

(15) 'I am wealthy and well-born. Who can match me? I shall sacrifice, I shall make donations, and I shall enjoy myself.' This is what those deluded by ignorance think.

(16) Bewildered by many thoughts, tangled in the web of delusion, obsessed with the gratification of desires, they fall into a contaminated hell.

(17) Self-obsessed, puffed up, filled with the arrogance and pride of wealth, they sacrifice in name only, fraudulently, without conforming to injunction.

(18) Depending on egotism, violence, pride, desire, and anger, these malcontents loathe me in their own bodies, and in those of others.

(19) Lowest of men—hating, vicious, and polluted; in the realms of rebirth I hurl them incessantly into truly demonic wombs.

(20) Cast into demonic wombs, deluded in birth after birth, failing to attain me, they go to the very lowest goal, Son of Kunti.

(21) Desire, anger, and greed: that is the destruction of the self, the triple gate of hell, so abandon those three.

(22) A man freed from these three gates of darkness approaches what is best for himself. So he goes to the highest goal, Son of Kunti.

(23) The man who, having abandoned the scriptural injunctions, follows his own desires, attains neither success, nor happiness, nor the highest goal.

(24) Scripture must therefore be your authority for determining what is to be done and what is not to be done. Having understood the prescribed scriptural teachings, you should perform actions here and now.

CHAPTER 17

Arjuna said:

(1) Those who, having abandoned the scriptural injunctions, sacrifice full of faith, how are they situated, Krishna? In purity, passion, or darkness?

The Lord said:

(2) The faith of the embodied is of three kinds: arising out of a person's own nature it is pure, passionate, or dark. Listen to this.

(3) In every case faith corresponds to one's nature, Bharata. A person is constructed by faith: whatever his faith is, so is he.

(4) The pure sacrifice to the gods, the passionate to spirits and demons; the others, men of darkness, sacrifice to disembodied spirits and the brood of malignant fiends.

(5–6) You should know that men who undertake extreme ascetic practices unsanctioned by scripture, in thrall to exhibitionism and egotism, driven by the forces of passion and desire, mindlessly emaciating the aggregate of elements that make up the body and me within the body, are set on the demonic.

(7) Again, everyone's preferred food is also of three kinds, as are sacrifice, asceticism, and gifts. Listen to how these are divided.

(8) The foods preferred by the pure increase life-span, well-being, strength, health, ease and pleasure; they are flavoursome, mild, firm-textured, and easy to digest.

(9) Foods desired by the passionate are pungent, bitter, salty, very hot, sharp, dry, and burning; they cause pain, anguish, and sickness.

(10) People of darkness prefer food that is raw, tasteless, putrid, left to stand overnight, leavings, and food rejected as unfit for sacrifice.

(11) That sacrificial offering is pure which is enjoined, which is made by those who have no desire for reward

and whose minds are concentrated on the injunction: 'This must be sacrificed.'

(12) But you should know, Greatest of Bharatas, that a sacrifice offered to obtain a reward, and for show, is passionate.

(13) Sacrifice devoid of proper injunctions, lacking distributed food, mantras, and sacrificial fees, and faithless, is governed by darkness.

(14) Bodily asceticism is said to consist of reverencing the gods, brahmins, teachers, and the wise, and of purity, honesty, continence, and non-violence.

(15) Vocal asceticism is said to consist of speech that does not cause distress, is truthful, pleasing, and beneficial, as well as the daily recitation of the sacred texts.

(16) Mental asceticism is said to consist of clarity of mind, gentleness, silence, self-control, and purity of disposition.

(17) That threefold asceticism, undertaken with utmost faith by disciplined men who have no desire for reward, is thought of as pure.

(18) Asceticism undertaken for the sake of honour, respect, reverence, and merely for show, is here categorized as passionate, unsteady, and impermanent.

(19) Asceticism practised with deluded notions, with self-torture, or with the object of destroying another person, is said to be dark in kind.

(20) A gift given, not in return for benefits received, but because it is one's duty to give to a worthy person at an appropriate time and place, is remembered as a pure donation.

(21) But that gift given with the purpose of returning a service, or with the hope of a reward later, and reluctantly, is remembered as passionate.

(22) That gift given offensively and contemptuously, at the wrong place and time, and to the unworthy, is said to be dark in kind.

(23) *Om tat sat:** this is committed to memory as the threefold designation of Brahman. Of old the brahmins, the Vedas, and the sacrifices were ordained by this.

(24) Therefore, for the propounders of Brahman, acts of sacrifice, donation, and asceticism, as prescribed in injunction, always begin after '*Om*' has been recited.

(25) Having pronounced '*tat*', acts of sacrifice and asceticism, and various acts of donation are performed without expectation of any reward by those who desire liberation.

(26) '*Sat*' is employed to designate 'what is' and 'the good'; the word '*sat*' is therefore used, Partha, for laudable action.

(27) And '*sat*', denoting 'steadfastness', is used for the sacrifice, asceticism, and donation; similarly, any action to those ends is also designated '*sat*'.

(28) An oblation offered, a gift given, an ascetic exercise undergone without faith is called '*asat*',* Partha; it has no significance, either here or hereafter.

CHAPTER 18

Arjuna said:

(1) Great Arm, Hrishikesha, Slayer of Keshin, I want to know the real nature of renunciation and abandonment, and how they differ.

The Lord said:

(2) Seers understand renunciation as the rejection of actions motivated by desires; the discerning describe abandonment as the giving up of the results of all actions.

(3) Some of the wise say that action is full of error and should be completely abandoned, others that actions such as sacrifice, giving, and asceticism should not be abandoned.

(4) Now Best of Bharatas, tiger of a man, hear my definitive statement concerning abandonment: abandonment is divided into three.

(5) Acts of sacrifice, giving, and asceticism should be undertaken, not abandoned. Sacrifice, giving, and asceticism purify the wise.

(6) But it is my final, definitive doctrine, Partha, that these actions should be undertaken only after attachment and interest in results have been abandoned.

(7) There should, however, be no renunciation of prescribed action; the deluded abandonment of that is a product of darkness.

(8) Whoever abandons an action because it is unpleasant, and out of fear of bodily affliction, has performed a passionate type of abandonment and does not obtain the reward of abandonment.

(9) Whoever undertakes controlled prescribed action, having abandoned all attachment and interest in its result, is considered, Arjuna, to have performed a pure kind of abandonment.

(10) The wise man, who has excised doubt, the abandoner filled with purity, neither recoils from an unpleasant action nor attaches himself to a pleasant one.

(11) For no embodied being can abandon actions completely; but it is the man who abandons the *result* of actions who is called 'abandoner'.

(12) For non-abandoners departing this life, the result of action is threefold: undesired, desired, and in between. But for renouncers there is none whatsoever.

(13) Great Arm, let me enlighten you: these five determinants are given in Sankhya doctrine* for the successful accomplishment of all actions:

(14) The locus of action, the agent, various material means, different kinds of actions, and fifth and last, divine fate.

(15) Whatever action a man undertakes with body, speech, and mind, whether proper or improper, these five are the causes of it.

(16) This being the case, the wrong-minded man, who, because his intelligence is inadequate, regards himself alone as the agent, sees nothing.

(17) For the man whose condition is not egoistical, and whose intelligence is not polluted, even though destroying these worlds, he does not kill and is not bound.

(18) Knowledge, the object of knowledge, and the knower are the threefold motivators of action; instrument, act, and agent comprise the action itself.

(19) According to the 'constituents of nature' theory, knowledge, action and agent are of three kinds, depending upon their constituents. Now hear about these as well.

(20) Know that knowledge by which one sees the one imperishable state of being in all creatures, the undivided among the divided, is purely constituted.

(21) And you should realize that that knowledge which sees a multiplicity of different states of being, separated among creatures, is passionately constituted.

(22) But that knowledge which, without reason, and lacking a true object, superficially fixes on a single effect as though it were everything, is said to be darkly constituted.

(23) That action which is prescribed, unaccompanied by attachment, undertaken without desire or aversion by one who is not interested in the result, is said to be purely constituted.

(24) But that action strained after with some desire in mind, out of egoism, is said to be passionately constituted.

(25) That action undertaken through delusion, reckless of consequence, death, or injury, ignoring one's human capacity, is said to be darkly constituted.

(26) The agent who is free from attachment and self-aggrandisement, resolute and persevering, the same in success and failure, is said to be purely constituted.

(27) The agent who is passionate, eager to obtain results from his actions, greedy, of a violent disposition, impure, and consumed by joy and grief, is said to be passionately constituted.

(28) The agent who is undisciplined, unrefined, stubborn, false, dishonest, idle, depressive, and procrastinating is said to be darkly constituted.

(29) Listen now to the threefold classification of intelligence and resolution, definitively and individually explained according to the constituents, Dhananjaya.

(30) That intelligence which knows about action and the cessation of action, what should be done and what should not be done, danger and security, bondage and liberation, is purely constituted, Partha.

(31) That intelligence which incorrectly perceives what is right and what is wrong, what should be done and what should not be done, is passionately constituted, Partha.

(32) That intelligence which, covered by darkness, believes what is wrong to be natural and good, and perverts everything, is darkly constituted, Partha.

(33) The resolution with which one controls the activities of the mind, the life breath, and the senses in unwavering yogic practice—that is purely constituted, Partha.

(34) Arjuna, the resolution with which one maintains order, pleasure, and prosperity, with attachment, desiring their fruits—that is passionately constituted, Partha.

(35) That resolution through which the fool will not give up sleep, fear, grief, depression, or intoxication is darkly constituted, Partha.

(36) But now, Bull of the Bharatas, hear me on the threefold happiness one enjoys through repeated practice, wherein one achieves an end to suffering.

(37) That happiness, born from the serenity of one's own intelligence, which to begin with seems like poison, and when developed is the most wonderful nectar, is said to be purely constituted.

(38) That happiness, arising from the contact of the senses with their objects, which to begin with seems like nectar, and when developed is like poison, is held to be passionately constituted.

(39) That happiness arising out of sleep, indolence, and negligence, which to begin with, and uninterruptedly thereafter, deludes the self, is said to be darkly constituted.

(40) There is no being, whether on earth or in heaven among the gods, that can be free from these three constituents, born of material nature.

(41) The actions of brahmins, of warriors and princes, of farmers and merchants, and of servants are all distributed according to the constituents that spring from their own natures, Incinerator of the Foe.*

(42) Serenity, self-restraint, asceticism, purity, patience, honesty, knowledge, insight, and religious faith are the actions of a brahmin, deriving from his own nature.

(43) Valour, vital power, resolution, skill, intransigence in battle, giving, and exercising power are the actions of warriors and princes, deriving from their own natures.

(44) Ploughing, tending cattle, and trade are the actions of farmers and merchants, deriving from their own natures; the essence of action for the servant is service, derived from his own nature.

(45) A man achieves perfection by contenting himself with his own work; hear how such a man, intent upon his own work, finds that perfection.

(46) A man attains perfection by reverencing, through his own specific activity, him from whom all creatures come into being, by whom all this is spread out.

(47) It is better to do one's own duty inadequately than another's well; no man is at fault performing an action enjoined by his own nature.

(48) Son of Kunti, a man should not abandon the work he was born into, even if it is faulty, for just as fire is wreathed in smoke all undertakings are attended by faults.

(49) A man whose intelligence is free of any attachment, who has conquered himself, whose desire has evaporated, attains the supreme perfection of freedom from action and its results through renunciation.

(50) Son of Kunti, learn from me in short how, having attained perfection, one also attains Brahman, which is the highest state of knowledge.

(51) Disciplined with a pure intelligence, having controlled the self with resolution, having abandoned sound and the other objects of the senses, and putting away attraction and aversion,

(52) Dwelling apart, eating little, controlling speech, body, and mind, continuously immersed in yogic concentration, cultivating dispassion,

(53) Having freed oneself from egoism, force, pride, desire, anger, and possessiveness, unselfish and serene, one is able to become Brahman.

(54) Having become Brahman, tranquil in the self, a man does not grieve and he does not desire; the same towards all creatures, he attains the highest devotion to me.

(55) Through devotion he recognizes me—how great I am, and who I am in reality; and then, having known me in reality, he enters me immediately.

(56) Though continually performing all actions, his refuge is in me, and through my grace he attains the eternal, imperishable home.

(57) Having surrendered in thought all your actions to me, holding me supreme, depending upon the yoga of intelligence, be ever thinking on me.

(58) For thinking on me, you shall by my grace sail past all obstacles; but if, falling into egoism, you pay no heed, you shall perish.

(59) If, falling into such egoism, you suppose you will not fight, your resolution is quite pointless: your material nature will constrain you.

(60) Bound by your own activity, which springs from your own nature, ineluctably, Son of Kunti, you will do precisely what, in your delusion, you try to avoid.

(61) Arjuna, in the centre of the heart of all beings their lord stands still, mechanically revolving all creatures through his magical power.

(62) Bharata, go with your whole being to him alone for refuge; through his grace you will reach supreme peace, eternal home.

(63) Such is the knowledge I have imparted to you, the mystery of mysteries; consider it fully, then do what you will.

(64) Beyond that, listen to my final word, the most secret of all. You have been assuredly singled out by me, so I shall speak it for your benefit.

(65) Fix your mind on me, devote yourself to me, sacrifice to me, do homage to me, and so you shall in reality come to me. I promise you: you are dear to me.

(66) Abandoning all duties, vow yourself to me alone. Don't agonize, I shall release you from all evils.

(67) You must never repeat this to one who neglects asceticism, to one who is not devoted, to one who has no desire to hear it, or to one who speaks ill of me.

(68) But he who propounds this supreme mystery to my devotees, having rendered the highest devotion to me, will, without a doubt, come to me.

(69) Among men there is no one who does more to please me than he, and no one on earth shall be dearer to me than he is.

(70) And I consider that he who commits this sacred dialogue of ours to memory, in effect worships me through a sacrifice of knowledge.

(71) And the man who listens to it, full of faith and without ill will, is also freed, and will attain the bright worlds of those whose actions have been meritorious.

(72) Partha, have you listened to this single-mindedly? Dhananjaya, has your delusion born of ignorance been dispelled?

Arjuna said:

(73) My delusion has been obliterated, and through your grace, Achyuta, I have remembered myself. I stand, my doubt dispelled. I shall do as you say.

Sanjaya said:

(74) Thus, shivers running down my spine, I have heard this astonishing dialogue between Vasudeva and the great-souled Partha.*

(75) By Vyasa's* grace, I have heard this supreme mystery, yoga, from Krishna, from the lord of yoga himself, who taught it directly.

(76) O King, repeatedly calling to mind this astounding, auspicious dialogue between Keshava and Arjuna, time and again I exult.

(77) And repeatedly calling to mind that more than astounding form of Hari,* I am greatly amazed, O King, and exult again and again.

(78) Wherever Krishna, the lord of yoga, and Partha, the bowman, are, I believe that there too there will be fortune, victory, prosperity, and lasting good counsel.

EXPLANATORY NOTES

1.1 **the Law**: the Sanskrit word is *dharma*. For some general remarks on this term see the Introduction. For notes on the *dramatis personae* see 'The Narrative Context' in the Introduction, and for an explanation of the typographical conventions used in Chapter 1 see p. xxv.

1.10 In common with a number of other translators and commentators I have departed from the critical edition here, transposing **Bhima** and **Bhisma**, and so giving the verse a more plausible sense. For another solution see Edgerton's translation.

1.35 **the three worlds**: heaven, earth, and the atmosphere or sometimes the lower regions.

1.37 **they are our own kinsmen**: taken against the critical edition's preferred text, which would translate the phrase as 'and their kinsmen'.

1.41 **the four estates**: according to classical Brahminical orthodoxy, human society is divided into four estates or classes: (1) brahmins or ritual specialists, (2) warriors and rulers, (3) merchants and farmers, (4) labourers and serfs. Membership of a particular estate, and so social status and function, is determined by birth and accords with natural law. Only male members of the three higher estates have access, via initiation (hence the epithet 'twice-born'), to the sacred texts and so to ritual. To disrupt this scheme is to fly in the face of natural law and so bring down evil on oneself and one's family.

1.42 **rice-ball and water offerings**: essential components of the rites performed to sustain the dead in the next world and specifically to ensure that the recently deceased makes the transfer from departed spirit to ancestor. It is the responsibility of the eldest son of the dead man to make these offerings. To do so he needs access to the sacred texts and therefore needs to belong to one of the three higher estates.

2.39 **Sankhya theory**: Sankhya theory has been utilized in one form or another by many schools of Indian thought, and it permeates the *Bhagavad Gita* (see especially Chapters 13 and 14). It is unlikely, however, that the term is used here (as it is later) to refer to an established philosophical school. Generally, it teaches that material nature (i.e. the universe and what it contains, including the physical and mental attributes of human beings) is a continuous process manifested in the dynamic interaction of three inextricably intertwined constituents, which are respectively pure, passionate, and dark. Of these, the pure constituent represents the principles of knowledge and freedom from pollution, the passionate those of activity and greed, the dark those of inertia and ignorance. The qualities of these constituents predominate to a greater or lesser degree in all material phenomena, and constrain beings to act in particular ways. Diametrically opposed to these constituents and to material nature as a whole, in the sense of belonging to a fundamentally different category (albeit the only other one in existence), are the 'spirits' or 'persons'. A 'person' is the passive and immutable self within a living creature, characterized by pure consciousness. In reality such 'persons' are totally distinct from material nature and are only involved with it because of the *embodied* person's ignorance of its true nature. In other words, it is the constituents of nature that act and experience the results of action; 'persons', on the other hand, in reality neither act nor experience the results, but through their contact with material nature are deluded into *supposing* that they do. Therein lies their bondage, and the reason why it seems to be real. Therefore it is knowledge of its true nature that, according to Sankhya theory, brings release for the essentially pure, unbound, and non-acting 'person'. In a theistic modification of this, material nature and its evolutes are said to comprise God's lower nature, while sentient beings constitute his higher nature (see, for example, *Bhagavad Gita* 7.4–5, and Chapters 13, 14, and 15 *passim*), a context in which 'persons' become 'Person' or the 'Self'.

2.42 **the Veda**: the revealed texts of Brahminical religion and mainstream Hinduism.

2.45 **the three constituents of material nature**: see note 2.39.

2.72 **the nirvana of Brahman**: 'nirvana' is a Buddhist term for the state that obtains when desire and its corollary, ignorance, have ceased to fuel the psychophysical entity that constitutes a 'person' and drive it on to further rebirth. It is a condition associated with deep coolness and peace. Its use here seems to be a deliberate attempt to upstage the Buddhist renouncers by linking that state of liberation with the supreme or absolute principle of the Upanishadic (and hence Vedic) tradition, Brahman. Cf. 5.24–26

3.3 **Sankhya theorists**: see note 2.39.

3.5 **the constituents which originate from material nature**: see note 2.39.

3.10 **Prajapati**: the 'Lord of Creatures', a name for the creator god according to Vedic cosmogony, protector of life and procreation.

3.15 **Brahman**: it seems that two meanings of this multivalent term are employed here: (1) Brahman as the Veda, its source being the imperishable syllable *Om*, which is thought to be a concentrate of the entire corpus; (2) Brahman as the all-pervading material cause of the creation.

3.17 **self**: i.e. the eternal, immutable essential self.

3.20 **King Janaka**: a legendary ruler of great piety; he appears in the *Brihadaranyaka Upanishad*.

3.22 **the three worlds**: see note 1.35.

3.42 **he**: the 'self' according to most commentators, although the eleventh century Vedantic philosopher, Ramanuja, takes it to refer to 'desire'.

4.1 **Vivasvat**: a sun god and the father of the original ancestor of the human race, **Manu. Ikshvaku** is one of Manu's sons.

4.13 **The four estates**: see note 1.41.

4.24 **Brahman**: here the supreme being and the totality of the sacrifice.

5.4 **the way of Sankhya**: i.e. the pursuit of liberating knowledge of reality, attained through renunciation. On Sankhya see note 2.39.

5.13 **nine-gated city**: the body.

5.24–26 **the nirvana of Brahman**: see note 2.72.

6.44 **the word-Brahman**: the Veda.

7.4–5 **lower nature . . . higher nature**: on this division see note 2.39.

7.19 **Vasudeva**: an epithet of Krishna.

8.13 **the one-syllabled Brahman, 'Om'**: see note 3.15.

8.16 **Brahma's realm**: the highest realm of transmigratory existence, but its occupants are still subject to death and rebirth.

8.17–18 According to a widely held cosmological view, time is divided into an infinite number of immensely long world cycles. Each cycle or **day of Brahma** is initiated by the emanation of all things from the unmanifest primal source and terminated by their reabsorption into it—only, after a **Brahma night**, for the process to be repeated in the next cycle.

8.24–25 These ideas about the passage of the self after death are derived from accounts in the two earliest *Upanishads*, the *Chandogya* (5.3 ff.) and the *Brihadaranyaka* (6.2 ff.).

9.7 **world cycle**: see note 8.17–18. Here Krishna identifies his material nature as the unmanifest source of all things.

9.17 **the Rig, the Sama, and the Yajur Vedas**: the three principal texts that constitute the Veda. The *Atharva Veda*, possibly a later addition, completes the corpus.

9.20 **soma-drinkers**: soma was the extract of a plant (also called soma) and a god. Offered and imbibed by the priests in the most elaborate and important of the Vedic sacrificial rituals, in its original form it was probably a hallucinogen. Its identity, however, was forgotten or lost, and it was replaced by (physically) non-intoxicating substitutes.

Indra: the chief Vedic deity.

10.6 **The ancient seven great seers and the four Manus**: the original ancestors. There is a Manu, a 'first man', at the beginning of each age.

10.12–13 **Vyasa**: the mythical author of the *Mahabharata*, and so of the *Bhagavad Gita*. The others are legendary seers and wise men. **Asita and Devala** may be two names of the same person.

10.20 In the next twenty verses Krishna identifies himself as the chief thing, essence, or prototype in all categories.

10.21 **Adityas**: Vedic celestial deities.

Maruts: storm gods.

10.22 **the mind**: the sixth sense, according to Sankhya theory.

10.23 **Rudras**: the 'roarers'; storm gods, sometimes identified with the Maruts.

Shiva: along with Vishnu and the Goddess, one of the supreme deities of medieval Hinduism. Under the name 'Rudra' he was connected with the Vedic Maruts or Rudras.

Lord of Wealth: Kubera or Kuvera, leader of the **Yakshas** and **Rakshasas**, classes of local spirits and demons.

Vasus: a class of atmospheric gods associated with the god Indra.

Meru: the mythical mountain at the centre of the universe.

10.24 **Brihaspati**: chief priest to the gods.

Skanda: the god of war.

10.26 **sacred fig tree**: see note 15.1.

Ghandarvas: celestial musicians.

10.27 **Ucchaihshravas, born from nectar**: the prototypical horse, created from nectar during the churning of the primeval ocean, according to a well-known cosmogonic myth.

10.29 **Ananta**: the 'endless'; the cosmic serpent upon which Vishnu sleeps in the interval between world cycles.

Varuna: one of the oldest Vedic gods, often connected with the waters.

Yama: the first man, and so the first to die, and therefore the god of the dead.

10.30 **Daityas**: a class of demons, opposed to the gods.

Prahlada: a Daitya who became a devotee of Vishnu.

Garuda: the bird on whom Vishnu rides.

10.31 **Rama**: either the hero of the epic *Ramayana* (Vishnu's seventh incarnation), or Parashu-Rama, Vishnu's sixth incarnation.

10.33 **the conjunctive one**: the reference is to a particular type of Sanskrit grammatical compound, one which can refer to many things.

10.34 **Of feminine things**: in Sanskrit these nouns are feminine in gender.

10.35 **Saman chants**: those employed in the *Sama Veda*.
Gayatri metre: a twenty-four syllable metre used in the *Rig Veda*.

10.37 **Vrishnis**: Krishna's clan or tribe.
Vasudeva: Krishna himself.
Vyasa: see note 10.12.
Ushanas: a famous Vedic seer-poet.

11.6 **Adityas**: see note 10.21.
Vasus: see note 10.23.
Rudras: see note 10.23.
Ashvins: twin gods who are skilled physicians.
Maruts: see note 10.21.

11.15 **Brahma**: the creator god.

11.20 **the three worlds**: see note 1.35.

11.22 **Rudras**: see note 10.23.
Adityas: see note 10.21.
Vasus: see note 10.23.
Sadhyas: a class of deities inhabiting the ether between heaven and earth.
Vishva gods: a particular troop of Vedic deities, but sometimes simply a term for all the gods.
Ashvins: see note 11.6.
steam-drinkers: a class of ancestors.
Yakshas: a type of semi-divine local spirit.
Asuras: a class of demons.

11.26 **sons of Dhritarashtra**: the Kauravas, Arjuna's opponents.
charioteer's son: Karna, a Kaurava general.

11.34 **Drona, etc.**: leading Kauravas and opponents of Arjuna, but also, of course, his kinsmen.

11.37 **Brahma**: see note 11.15.

11.39 **Vayu**: the Vedic wind god.
Yama: see note 10.29.
Agni: the god of fire.
Varuna: see note 10.29.
Prajapati: see note 3.10.

great grandfather: primal ancestor.

11.46 **four-armed**: a standard iconographic depiction of Vishnu (i.e. Krishna).

13.5 In this Sankhya classification the **gross elements** are earth, water, fire, air, and ether (space); the **eleven faculties** are hearing, seeing, touching, tasting, smelling, plus mind and the five motor organs: hands, feet, mouth (voice), anus, and genitals; the **five realms of the senses** are sound, colour, touch, taste, and smell.

13.24 **Sankhya**: see note 2.39.

15.1 **Ashvattha**: a sacred fig tree; here used as an image for the cosmos, i.e. the whole universe of birth, death, and rebirth, from which, ultimately, liberation is sought.

15.13 **Soma**: see note 9.20.

15.15 **Vedanta**: 'the end of the Veda', i.e. the *Upanishads*, a group of texts belonging to the Veda which teach, among other things, liberation from rebirth through knowledge of the identity of the microcosm and the macrocosm, the inner self and Brahman.

17.23 ***Om tat sat***: the literal 'meaning' of this Sanskrit mantra is '*Om*—that—it is.'

17.28 ***asat***: the negative of *sat*, so 'it is not.'

18.13 **Sankhya doctrine**: see note 2.39.

18.41 See note 1.41.

18.74 **Vasudeva and . . . Partha**: Krishna and Arjuna.

18.75 **Vyasa**: see note 10.12–13.

18.77 **Hari**: Vishnu (Krishna).

NOTE ON THE PRONUNCIATION OF SANSKRIT NAMES

In the translation and introduction I have avoided the use of diacritical marks when using Sanskrit terms and proper names. So the name *Dhṛtarāṣṭra*, for instance, has been spelt 'Dhritarashtra'. (In the Introduction some terms have been anglicized: 'brahmin' for *brāhman* (a priest), and so 'Brahminical' instead of 'Brahmanical', etc.) This gives an approximate guide to pronunciation, although there is no indication where a vowel should be lengthened. For those interested in attaining a greater degree of accuracy the following may act as a guide, but for detailed information on the pronunciation of Sanskrit the reader should consult chapter 1 of Michael Coulson's *Sanskrit: An Introduction to the Classical Language* (Teach Yourself Books, 1992).

Pronounce Sanskrit	as in English
a	c*u*t
ā	f*a*r
i	s*i*t
ī	m*e*
u	p*u*t
ū	t*oo*
ṛ	*r*isk
e	pr*ay*
ai	s*i*gh
o	h*o*pe
au	s*ou*nd
c	*ch*urch
v	close to the English *w*
ś	*sh*ame
ṣ	di*sh*

Pronounce Sanskrit	as in English
ḥ	as in English, but with a faint echo of the preceding vowel
ṭ etc.	as in English, but with the tongue further back in the mouth
ṅ, ṇ	have a nasal quality
ñ,	ca*ny*on
kh, gh, ch, jh, ṭh, ḍh, th, dh, ph, bh	aspirated, as in 'ho*th*ouse', *not* 'wi*th*', 'she*ph*erd', 'clu*bh*ouse', etc.
ṃ	nasalizes the preceding vowel sound, as in French *bon*

LIST OF SANSKRIT NAMES AND TERMS

An alphabetically arranged list of the Sanskrit names and terms occurring in the text and introduction, with (where appropriate) their diacritical equivalents, is given below.

Word as spelt in the text	Equivalent with diacritical marks
Achyuta	Acyuta
Aditya	Āditya
Agni	Agni
Airavata	Airāvata
Ananta	Ananta
Anantavijaya	Anantavijaya
Arjuna	Arjuna
Aryaman	Aryaman
asat	asat
Ashvattha	Aśvattha
Ashvatthaman	Aśvatthāman
Asita	Asita
Asvin	Aśvin
Atharva	Atharva
avatara	avatāra
Bhagavad Gita	Bhagavad Gītā
Bharata	Bharata
Bharata	Bhārata (descendant of Bharata)
Bhima	Bhīma
Bhisma	Bhīṣma
Bhrigu	Bhṛgu
Brahma	Brahmā
Brahman	brahman
brahmin	brāhman (priest)
Brihadaranyaka	Bṛhadāraṇyaka
Brihaspati	Bṛhaspati
Chandogya	Chāndogya

Word as spelt in the text	Equivalent with diacritical marks
Chekitana	Cekitāna
Chitraratha	Citraratha
Daitya	Daitya
Devadatta	Devadatta
Devala	Devala
Dhananjaya	Dhanaṃjaya
Dharma	Dharma
Dhrishtadyumna	Dhṛṣṭadyumna
Dhrishtaketu	Dhṛṣṭaketu
Dhritarashtra	Dhṛtarāṣṭra
Draupadi	Draupadī
Drona	Droṇa
Drupada	Drupada
Duryodhana	Duryodhana
Dvaraka	Dvārakā
Gandharva	Gandharva
Gandiva	Gāṇḍīva
Garuda	Garuḍa
Gayatri	Gāyatrī
Govinda	Govinda
Gudakesha	Guḍākeśa
Hari	Hari
Himalaya	Himālaya
Hrishikesha	Hṛṣīkeśa
Ikshvaku	Ikṣvāku
Indra	Indra
Janaka	Janaka
Janardana	Janārdana
Jayadratha	Jayadratha
Kandarpa	Kandarpa
Kapila	Kapila
karma	karma
Karna	Karṇa
Kashi	Kāśi
Kaurava	Kaurava
Keshava	Keśava

Word as spelt in the text	Equivalent with diacritical marks
Keshin	Keśin
Kripa	Kṛpa
Krishna	Kṛṣṇa
Kubera/Kuvera	Kubera/Kuvera
Kunti	Kuntī
Kuntibhoja	Kuntibhoja
Kuru	Kuru
Madhava	Mādhava
Madhu	Madhu
Madhusudana	Madhusūdana
Mahabharata	Mahābhārata
Manipushpaka	Maṇipuṣpaka
Manu	Manu
Marichi	Marīci
Marut	Marut
Meru	Meru
Naga	Nāga
Nakula	Nakula
Narada	Nārada
nirvana	nirvāṇa
Om	Oṃ
Om tat sat	Oṃ tat sat
Panchajanya	Pāñcajanya
Pandava	Pāṇḍava
Pandu	Pāṇḍu
Parashu-Rama	Paraśu-Rāma
Partha	Pārtha
Paundra	Pauṇḍra
Prahlada	Prahlāda
Prajapati	Prajāpati
Purujit	Purujit
Rakshasa	Rākṣasa
Rama	Rāma
Ramanuja	Rāmānuja
Ramayana	Rāmāyaṇa
Rig	Ṛg

Word as spelt in the text	Equivalent with diacritical marks
Rudra	Rudra
Sadhya	Sādhya
Sahadeva	Sahadeva
Sama	Sāma
Saman	Sāman
Sanjaya	Saṃjaya
Sankhya	Sāṃkhya
Satyaki	Sātyaki
Savyasachin	Savyasācin
Shaibya	Śaibya
Shankara	Śaṅkara
Shikhandin	Śikhaṇḍin
Shiva	Śiva
shloka	śloka
Skanda	Skanda
soma	soma
Somadatta	Somadatta
Subhadra	Subhadrā
Sughosha	Sughoṣa
trishtubh	triṣṭubh
Ucchaihshravas	Ucchaiḥśravas
Upanishad	Upaniṣad
Ushanas	Uśanas
Uttamaujas	Uttamaujas
Vaishnava	Vaiṣṇava
Varshneya	Vārṣṇeya
Varuna	Varuṇa
Vasu	Vasu
Vasudeva	Vāsudeva
Vasuki	Vāsuki
Vayu	Vāyu
Veda	Veda
Vedanta	Vedānta
Vedantin	Vedāntin
Vikarna	Vikarṇa
Virata	Virāṭa

Word as spelt in the text	Equivalent with diacritical marks
Vishnu	Viṣṇu
Vishva	Viśva
Vivasvat	Vivasvat
Vrishni	Vṛṣṇi
Vyasa	Vyāsa
Yadava	Yādava
Yajur	Yajur
Yaksha	Yakṣa
Yama	Yama
Yoga	yoga
Yudhamanyu	Yudhāmanyu
Yudhishthira	Yudhiṣṭhira
Yuyudhana	Yuyudhāna

THE WORLD'S CLASSICS

A Select List

HANS ANDERSEN: Fairy Tales
Translated by L. W. Kingsland
Introduction by Naomi Lewis
Illustrated by Vilhelm Pedersen and Lorenz Frølich

ARTHUR J. ARBERRY (Transl.): The Koran

LUDOVICO ARIOSTO: Orlando Furioso
Translated by Guido Waldman

ARISTOTLE: The Nicomachean Ethics
Translated by David Ross

JANE AUSTEN: Emma
Edited by James Kinsley and David Lodge

Northanger Abbey, Lady Susan, The Watsons, *and* Sanditon
Edited by John Davie

Persuasion
Edited by John Davie

WILLIAM BECKFORD: Vathek
Edited by Roger Lonsdale

KEITH BOSLEY (Transl.): The Kalevala

CHARLOTTE BRONTË: Jane Eyre
Edited by Margaret Smith

JOHN BUNYAN: The Pilgrim's Progress
Edited by N. H. Keeble

FRANCES HODGSON BURNETT: The Secret Garden
Edited by Dennis Butts

FANNY BURNEY: Cecilia or Memoirs of an Heiress
Edited by Peter Sabor and Margaret Anne Doody

THOMAS CARLYLE: The French Revolution
Edited by K. J. Fielding and David Sorensen

LEWIS CARROLL: Alice's Adventures in Wonderland
and Through the Looking Glass
Edited by Roger Lancelyn Green
Illustrated by John Tenniel

MIGUEL DE CERVANTES: Don Quixote
Translated by Charles Jarvis
Edited by E. C. Riley

GEOFFREY CHAUCER: The Canterbury Tales
Translated by David Wright

ANTON CHEKHOV: The Russian Master and Other Stories
Translated by Ronald Hingley

JOHN CLELAND:
Memoirs of a Woman of Pleasure (Fanny Hill)
Edited by Peter Sabor

WILKIE COLLINS: Armadale
Edited by Catherine Peters

JOSEPH CONRAD: Chance
Edited by Martin Ray

Victory
Edited by John Batchelor
Introduction by Tony Tanner

NORMAN DAVIS (Ed.): The Paston Letters

CHARLES DICKENS: Christmas Books
Edited by Ruth Glancy

Sikes and Nancy and Other Public Readings
Edited by Philip Collins

FEDOR DOSTOEVSKY: Crime and Punishment
Translated by Jessie Coulson
Introduction by John Jones

ARTHUR CONAN DOYLE:
Sherlock Holmes: Selected Stories
Introduction by S. C. Roberts

ALEXANDRE DUMAS *père*:
The Three Musketeers
Edited by David Coward

ALEXANDRE DUMAS *fils*:
La Dame aux Camélias
Translated by David Coward

MARIA EDGEWORTH: Castle Rackrent
Edited by George Watson

GEORGE ELIOT:
Felix Holt, The Radical
Edited by Fred C. Thompson

Middlemarch
Edited by David Carroll

Scenes of Clerical Life
Edited by Thomas A. Noble

Selected Critical Writings
Edited by Rosemary Ashton

GUSTAVE FLAUBERT: Madame Bovary
Translated by Gerard Hopkins
Introduction by Terence Cave

BENJAMIN FRANKLIN: Autobiography and other Writings
Edited by Ormond Seavey

ELIZABETH GASKELL: Cousin Phillis and Other Tales
Edited by Angus Easson

My Lady Ludlow and Other Stories
Edited by Edgar Wright

J. W. VON GOETHE: Faust, Part One
Translated by David Luke

OLIVER GOLDSMITH: The Vicar of Wakefield
Edited by Arthur Friedman

THOMAS HARDY: A Pair of Blue Eyes
Edited by Alan Manford

HESIOD: Theogony *and* Works and Days
Translated by M. L. West

E. T. A. HOFFMANN: The Golden Pot and Other Tales
Translated and Edited by Ritchie Robertson

HOMER: The Iliad
Translated by Robert Fitzgerald
Introduction by G. S. Kirk

THOMAS HUGHES: Tom Brown's Schooldays
Edited by Andrew Sanders

HENRIK IBSEN: An Enemy of the People, The Wild Duck, Rosmersholm
Edited and Translated by James McFarlane

HENRY JAMES: The Ambassadors
Edited by Christopher Butler

M. R. JAMES: Casting the Runes and Other Ghost Stories
Edited by Michael Cox

JOCELIN OF BRAKELOND:
Chronicle of the Abbey of Bury St. Edmunds
Translated by Diana Greenway and Jane Sayers

GWYN JONES (Transl.):
Eirik the Red and Other Icelandic Sagas

BEN JONSON: Five Plays
Edited by G. A. Wilkes

MADAME DE LAFAYETTE: The Princesse de Clèves
Translated and Edited by Terence Cave

WILLIAM LANGLAND: Piers Plowman
Translated and Edited by A. V. C. Schmidt

J. SHERIDAN LE FANU: Uncle Silas
Edited by W. J. McCormack

MIKHAIL LERMONTOV: A Hero of our Time
Translated by Vladimar Nabokov with Dmitri Nabokov

MATTHEW LEWIS: The Monk
Edited by Howard Anderson

MARCUS AURELIUS: The Meditations of Marcus Aurelius
Translated by A. S. L. Farquharson
Edited by R. B. Rutherford

KATHERINE MANSFIELD: Selected Stories
Edited by D. M. Davin

CHARLES MATURIN: Melmoth the Wanderer
Edited by Douglas Grant
Introduction by Chris Baldick

HERMAN MELVILLE: The Confidence-Man
Edited by Tony Tanner

Moby Dick
Edited by Tony Tanner

PROSPER MÉRIMÉE: Carmen and Other Stories
Translated by Nicholas Jotcham

MICHELANGELO: Life, Letters, and Poetry
Translated by George Bull with Peter Porter

MOLIÈRE: Don Juan and Other Plays
Translated by George Graveley and Ian Maclean

E. NESBIT: The Railway Children
Edited by Dennis Butts

EDGAR ALLAN POE: Selected Tales
Edited by Julian Symons

JEAN RACINE: Britannicus, Phaedra, Athaliah
Translated by C. H. Sisson

ANN RADCLIFFE: The Italian
Edited by Frederick Garber

THE MARQUIS DE SADE:
The Misfortune of Virtue and Other Early Tales
Translated and Edited by David Coward

SIR WALTER SCOTT: The Heart of Midlothian
Edited by Claire Lamont

ANNA SEWELL: Black Beauty
Edited by Peter Hollindale

TOBIAS SMOLLETT: The Expedition of Humphry Clinker
Edited by Lewis M. Knapp
Revised by Paul-Gabriel Boucé

ROBERT LOUIS STEVENSON:
Treasure Island
Edited by Emma Letley

ANTHONY TROLLOPE: The American Senator
Edited by John Halperin

GIORGIO VASARI: The Lives of the Artists
Translated and Edited by Julia Conaway Bondanella and Peter Bondanella

VIRGINIA WOOLF: Orlando
Edited by Rachel Bowlby

ÉMILE ZOLA: Nana
Translated and Edited by Douglas Parmée